CHAKRAS FOR BEGINNERS

Awaken Your Spiritual Power by Balancing and Healing the 7 Chakras With Self-Healing Techniques

EMILY ODDO

CONTENTS

Introduction	vii
1. THE CHAKRAS AND THEIR PROPERTIES	1
The Chakras	1
Symptoms of Chakra Imbalance	17
What Causes Chakra Imbalance?	22
2. BENEFITS OF CHAKRA HEALING	28
What Is Chakra Healing?	28
The Benefits of Healing Your Chakras	29
3. MEDITATION AND CHAKRA HEALING TECHNIQUES	35
Yoga and Exercise	35
Meditation	52
Visualization	68
Affirmations	70
Massage	80
Color Therapy	84
Musical Healing	88
Reiki	91
4. FOODS AND CHAKRAS	92
The Relationship Between Chakras and Food	93
Detoxing and Fasting	100
5. ESSENTIAL OILS AND CHAKRAS	104
Aromatherapy	105
Essential Oils for Chakra Healing	107
Where to Use Our Chakra Oils	109

6. CRYSTALS AND CHAKRAS — 113
   Crystals for Chakra Healing — 113
   Setting up for Crystal Healing — 123
   Using Crystals in Our Daily Lives — 125

7. THINGS YOU NEED TO KNOW — 128
   FAQ — 128

8. OTHER BOOKS BY THE AUTHOR — 131

   Afterword — 133
   References — 135

© **Copyright 2021 - All rights reserved.**

The content contained within this book may not be reproduced, duplicated or transmitted without direct written permission from the author or the publisher.

Under no circumstances will any blame or legal responsibility be held against the publisher, or author, for any damages, reparation, or monetary loss due to the information contained within this book, either directly or indirectly.

Legal Notice:

This book is copyright protected. It is only for personal use. You cannot amend, distribute, sell, use, quote or paraphrase any part, or the content within this book, without the consent of the author or publisher.

Disclaimer Notice:

Please note the information contained within this document is for educational and entertainment purposes only. All effort has been executed to present accurate, up to date, reliable, complete information. No warranties of any kind are declared or implied. Readers acknowledge that the author is not engaged in the rendering of legal, financial, medical or professional advice. The content within this book has been derived from various sources. Please consult a licensed professional before attempting any techniques outlined in this book.

By reading this document, the reader agrees that under no circumstances is the author responsible for any losses, direct or indirect, that are incurred as a result of the use of the information contained within this document, including, but not limited to, errors, omissions, or inaccuracies.

INTRODUCTION

WHAT ARE CHAKRAS?

What are chakras? This is a question that may have many different answers depending on who you ask. The word chakra comes from the Pali word *cakka* which means "wheel". As early as 2500 BCE, we have evidence of the wheel symbol used by the Indus Valley civilization to signify the sun, light, and knowledge. Traditionally, chakras have been an important part of three of the great ancient Indian religions, Hinduism, Buddhism, and Jainism. We may never know when the ancients first discovered the concept of chakras as energy centers, but we can trace their earliest mention back to medieval Hindu and Tantric Buddhist texts.

Buddhism

The eighth-century Buddhist texts, the Hevajra Tantra and the Caryagiti, both mention four centers of powerful inner energy stored in the core of the body. These are the first mentions we know of chakras as a center of power in the body. The words *cakka* (wheel), *pitha* (mound), and *padma* (lotus) are used interchangeably to describe these energy centers in the texts.

One of the core beliefs of Buddhism is the Dharmachakra. The Dharmachakra tells the story of Gautama Buddha's journey to enlightenment by preaching his message. Buddha supposedly set in motion the "wheel of dharma", and by doing so, he started bringing great change to the world.

The usage of a wheel metaphor and symbol stems from the Hindu myth of the *chakravartin* (wheel-turner). The chakravartin is the ideal king—a leader in possession of many great tools, including a wheel with which he can move his empire effortlessly in any direction. Although this is not exactly the chakra we know and want to learn about in this book, it's important to understand the origin of this ancient term.

The chakras in our bodies are powerful driving forces. With enough discipline and practice, we can use them to get closer to enlightenment. We can become our *own* chakravartin, driving ourselves toward success, happiness, and knowledge.

A wheel turning symbolizes the cycle of life in Buddhism. These constant cycles of birth and death, health and sickness, and suffering and happiness are defining features of Buddhist doctrine. Similarly, and possibly because of this symbolism, the chakras in our bodies are visualized as spinning wheels of energy.

Hinduism

In Tantric Hinduism, the *Kubjikamata* and *Kaulajnananirnaya* are the first texts we know of which include chakras as bodily energy sources. These texts, which were written between the first and fifth centuries CE, took the Buddhist concept of four chakras and built on it significantly, adding thousands of minor chakras and increasing the amount of primary chakras up to seven.

In the first millennium CE, following Hinduism's expansion of the chakra concept, Hindu scholars and religious leaders started to explore and document chakras more comprehensively. Over the coming centuries, a clear central belief was built around the energy points. According to Hinduism, human life exists in two parallel planes of existence: the physical (*sthula sarira*) and the emotional or psychological, which is also called the subtle (*sukshma sarira*).

The subtle is made up from energy that drives our emotions, intelligent thought, and conscious being. The physical, on the other hand, is made up from the physical body and world we inhabit. The physical and subtle influence and affect each other mutually. The subtle body can be described as paths of energy called *nadi*, which are connected to centers of power that are our chakras.

CHAPTER 1
THE CHAKRAS AND THEIR PROPERTIES

THE CHAKRAS

Root Chakra

The root chakra is also known as the Muladhara, which is Sanskrit for "root and basis of existence". This is the first of the seven chakras that we will be covering in this chapter. The root chakra is located at the base of the spine and the pelvic floor. Inactive Kundalini is said to be found residing in this chakra. Kundalini is power from the divine feminine, the mother goddess. This power resides inside each person. By unblocking and opening each chakra, this power will rise until it reaches our crown chakra. Once Kundalini has reached the crown chakra, we will experience enlightenment.

Think of this first chakra as the roots of a great tree. This tree grows tall and wide with plenty of fruit-laden branches. The Muladhara provides us with a solid base, an intimate connection to the earth and the ground around us, and the stability needed for us to grow. This chakra also has a strong connection to the things we need to ground ourselves. Our basic human needs of food, water, shelter, and feelings of love and safety are the most important grounding elements in our lives. Once these needs have been satisfied, we are much more likely to be content and comfortable. This chakra can also associate itself with the need to be fearless and face our worries.

The earth element is heavily associated with this chakra and also the color red, which symbolizes soil, rock, and clay, the building blocks of our world. This chakra is symbolized by a red lotus with four petals and a yellow square at its center. On each petal is a Sanskrit syllable which represents the four aspects of consciousness associated with this chakra. These syllables are vaṃ (joy), ṣaṃ (control), saṃ (concentration), and śaṃ (pleasure). The center syllable of this chakra is laṃ (Pride). The god Indra, deity of heaven, rain, and war, is most associated with this chakra. His western equivalents can be seen as Zeus, Jupiter, and Thor.

Sacral Chakra

The sacral chakra is also known as the Svadhisthana, Sanskrit for "where the self is established". It is the second of the seven chakras. We'll find this one at the base of the sexual organs. The sacral chakra is the source of sexual desire, and it is believed that this may be the hardest chakra to unblock for those wishing to raise their Kundalini through it. Think of this energy point as the lowest branches of the great tree. These branches take time to develop and are the first to bear fruit. This chakra takes much meditation and discipline to balance, but once it is done, the rewards are plentiful.

This second chakra provides us with our sexual energy, pleasure, sensuality, and sense of intimacy. The Svadhisthana is the first place our Kundalini will travel toward once awakened. This is the source of our love and fertility, two of the core aspects of the mother goddess. This chakra has a strong connection to many emotional aspects of our relationships with other people and is responsible for our ability to give and receive love, intimacy, and sexual energy. One who masters meditation on it can obtain mental clarity, a strengthened natural charisma, and increased confidence.

The element of water is representative of this chakra with its healing, flowing, and life-giving properties. The color associated with this chakra is orange, which symbolizes joy, activity, and energy. The Svadhisthana is naturally a chakra of great physical activity and vigor. Orange serves to visualize the energy of the sun and world around us, which helps to feed the energy in this chakra.

It is symbolized by a six-petaled orange lotus with a silver crescent moon sitting horizontally in the bottom-center. Each petal contains the Sanskrit syllables representing six aspects of consciousness that are related to this chakra and must be overcome. These syllables are baṃ (possessiveness), maṃ (destructiveness), bhaṃ (pitilessness), laṃ (suspicion), yaṃ (delusion), and raṃ (disdain). The center syllable of this chakra is vaṃ (joy).

Two gods are most associated with this chakra, including the creator of the universe Brahma and the god of knowledge Saraswati. Brahma can be likened to the Abrahamic monotheistic God, Yahweh or Allah. Brahma is viewed as the great creator and father, which explains his link to this chakra that is involved so heavily in reproduction. On the other hand, Saraswati is more closely related to Apollo the Greek and Roman god of music and knowledge. Along with being a center for sexual energy, this chakra is also a hub for creativity and personal knowledge. Saraswati represents the creative energy and inner knowledge one can release through meditation on the sacral chakra.

Solar Plexus Chakra

Our third chakra is the solar plexus, or Manipura, chakra. Manipura translates to "resplendent gem". This center of power is located just above the navel in the complicated network of nerves that makes up the solar plexus. The Manipura chakra is responsible for our dynamism, power of will, inner strength, and sense of achievement. This chakra is believed to be the source of all "prana" that we produce. Prana is the all-permeating essential lifeforce of the world that powers our body.

While the root chakra makes up the roots of a great tree and the sacral chakra makes up the fruit-bearing branches, the solar plexus chakra is the xylem or pith. The xylem in every tree are the soft core cells which are responsible for transporting nutrients around the tree and providing it with the energy needed to grow. This chakra is heavily associated with energy and forces of change. It is said to drive our metabolism and influence the powers of transformation that come naturally to us. It radiates into our other chakras as well and enhances the emotions connected to them.

An opened Manipura will enhance the love felt in the Anahata chakra above it, increase the sensuality felt in the Svadhisthana below it, and empower the strength down in the Muladhara chakra, among other things. In essence, it acts as the source of all positivity which drives the positive aspects of every chakra. By meditating on the Manipura, one positively improves all aspects of their being.

The Manipura chakra is most associated with the element of fire. This energetic and transformative element perfectly signifies the aspects most important to the Manipura. This chakra is visualized as a red downward triangle surrounded by a yellow circle, with ten darker-colored petals along its edges. Yellow is the color most associated with this chakra and the inner flame which it radiates throughout the body.

Contained within the petals are ten syllables that represent the ten aspects of this chakra which must be overcome in order to proceed. These syllables are phaṁ (sadness), ḍaṁ (narrowmindedness), naṁ (delusion), paṁ (foolishness), ḍhaṁ (greed), ṇaṁ (jealousy), taṁ (treachery), daṁ (fear), dhaṁ (disgust), and thaṁ (shame).

The two deities most associated with this chakra are Vishnu the god of protection and Lakshmi the god of prosperity. Vishnu is one of the three most powerful gods in Hinduism, alongside Brahma and Shiva. His primary role is that of a protector and god of change. Some similar gods to Vishnu from different regions are Tyr, the norse god of justice and protection, and Horus, the Egyptian god of the sky and protection. Lakshmi is one of the three most powerful female goddesses in Hinduism, along with Saraswati and Parvati. She represents wealth, beauty, and health and is considered the mother goddess of Hinduism. Her western equivalent could be seen as Hera, the queen of the greek pantheon.

Heart Chakra

The fourth chakra on our journey to enlightenment is the heart chakra, or Anahata. Anahata is Sanskrit for "unhurt, unstruck, and unbeaten". This name stems from the Vedic idea of Anahata Nad, which means the unstruck sound, or the sound which emanates from the celestial realm. Although called the heart chakra, the Anahata is actually in the center of our chest, just behind our heart. The heart chakra is responsible for our ability to make decisions of a higher nature.

Every chakra below the Anahata is bound by the rules of karma and fate. The bottom three chakras are dictated by earthly desires and emotions. On the other hand, the heart chakra is dictated by one's higher consciousness. With an open Anahata, we can make decisions on a spiritual level rather than at the level of a lower human. Just like with the heartwood of a tree which protects the plant from decay and rot, the heart chakra protects us from spiritual decay and falling victim to our base desires.

The heart chakra is most associated with love, compassion, balance, and inner peace. It is believed that this chakra acts as the middle ground between our spiritual and physical selves. It helps to integrate and accommodate for our base desires and our spiritual needs. Inner peace can be achieved once one opens the Anahata chakra and balances their desires and needs from both a spiritual and physical standpoint. This chakra acts as a mediator between our two aspects of self and allows us to follow our heart and make decisions for the betterment of our higher self.

The Anahata is closely linked to the element of air, and like the wind, the love from this chakra flows through and around everything it comes into contact with. This chakra is visualized as a lotus flower with twelve petals. In the center of this flower are two intersecting triangles that form a six-pointed star. This symbol represents the union of woman and man, as well as the union of body and spirit. The color of this chakra and its symbols is green. The reason that green is the color of this chakra is that it is the color most associated with safety, abundance, and health. These qualities are equally important for our physical and spiritual selves.

In the twelve petals around the edge of the lotus lay twelve syllables that are representative of the twelve divine qualities of the heart. These syllables include kam (bliss), kham (peace), gam (harmony), gham (love), ngam (understanding), cham (empathy), chham (clarity), jam (purity), jham (unity), nyam (compassion), tam (kindness), and tham (forgiveness). These twelve divine qualities have twelve counterparts that one must discard and overcome in order to fully open their Anahata. They are asha (desire), cinta (worry), cesta (struggle), mamta (possessiveness), dhamba (vanity), viveka (discrimination), vikalata (depression), ahamkara (pride), lolata (selfishness), kapatata (hypocrisy), vitarka (indecision), and anutapa (guilt).

Lastly, this chakra is heavily linked to the deity Vayu, the god of air and wind. Vayu is also seen as the god in control of breathing, therefore he is often considered the giver of life. His western counterpart is Amun, the Egyptian god of creation and wind.

Throat Chakra

The throat chakra is our fifth chakra and is also known as the Vishuddha chakra. The word Vishuddha translates to "especially pure". This name stems from the fact that the purity and openness of this energy point is incredibly important for all aspects of our life. This is the first of the three spiritual chakras, meaning that this chakra has more power over our spiritual forms than our physical forms. Although it is known as the throat chakra, it is actually based in the region of our larynx. The Vishuddha chakra is responsible for our ability to take words, thoughts, and ideas and turn them into reality. This chakra is the home of our creativity and the willpower needed to make thoughts a reality.

For example, someone with a blocked throat chakra may complain about their job all day but never have the willpower to make a change. Those who open their throat chakra have the ability to make the changes they want in life. Humans are unique in needing to open this chakra for themselves.

If we observe plants and animals, we can see that they never think twice about doing what they believe is best for them. Trees always grow toward the light at the top of the canopy, and animals always do whatever they must to survive. Humans are the only creatures that need to work toward having that willpower to turn their desires into reality.

The throat chakra is most commonly associated with expression, creativity, our connection to other realms, purpose, and the ability to learn from mistakes. It is believed that this chakra is the source of our independence. Only we control our lives and this chakra, when open, affords us the knowledge, wisdom, and willpower to do that. In connection with the third eye chakra, this is where we discover our purpose in life. Just as the heart chakra before this allows us to follow our heart and make decisions for our higher self, this chakra gives us the tools and power to follow through with those decisions.

The Vishuddha chakra is most commonly associated with the elements of space and sound. Space provides us with the room to grow and expand on a psychological level, and sound is needed for us to speak our minds and hear new lessons. This chakra is visualized as a white lotus flower with sixteen violet petals. Violet and blue are the primary colors for this energy point. Within this lotus is a blue downward-facing triangle and within that triangle is a circle. Inside the lotus below the triangle is an upward-facing half-moon. The sixteen petals around the lotus contain syllables that represent the sixteen siddhis (powers) that one can attain through meditation. Included in these sixteen powers are abilities such as immunity to hunger and thirst, perfect balance and health, out-of-body experiences, and influencing others.

This chakra is linked to the deity Shiva, specifically his form of panchavaktra with five heads and four arms. An ancient Hindu story recalls how in a struggle between the gods and a great serpent, the world was put at risk by the poison the beast spewed from its fangs. Desperate to save the world, the gods gathered all the poison into a bowl, but they couldn't figure out how to dispose of it. Lord Shiva, ever gracious, decided that he would risk his life and drink the poison. He emptied the bowl, but instead of drinking the poison down his throat, he held it there in the Vishuddha chakra and purified it into water. In this way, he saved the world from certain destruction.

Shiva is a unique deity with many aspects that make it hard to compare him with deities from other pantheons. The closest comparison we may get is Osiris from the Egyptian pantheon; they both share very polarizing roles in being protectors and guardians of man while being very violent deities.

Third Eye Chakra

The third eye chakra is the sixth and second-last chakra that will feature in this chapter. This chakra is also known as Ajna which translates to "perception" and "command". This name comes from the fact that this chakra is believed to be the force which guides us in life. It houses our intuition and subconscious wisdom. As the name suggests, this chakra is based in the center of our brow just above our eyes. It is tradition for many Jain and Hindu worshippers to place a bright red bindi (colored dot) on their forehead to show their admiration for this chakra.

The Ajna chakra is responsible for our ability to connect to the spiritual side of the world. It is said that someone with an opened third eye chakra can receive messages from the past and future. Whether we know it or not, this energy point plays a major role in guiding us through our lives. Even those with a closed third eye will still occasionally receive messages of great importance; these are the gut feelings and unexplainable pulls towards decisions that we sometimes feel.

This chakra is most associated with knowledge, intuition, perception of our world and others, wisdom, inspiration, and spiritual leadership. It is not only responsible for guiding us in our times of need, but those with an opened third eye are capable of spiritually guiding others toward enlightenment. Once one opens their third eye, they gain the ability to act as a spiritual lightning rod. They will behave like a magnet for wisdom and premonition, being able to guide themselves and others through times of spiritual uncertainty. The Ajna also directly affects our ability to detect lies. Thus, those with an opened third eye are far more aware of the truths of the world around them.

The third eye chakra is closely linked to what is known as the "supreme element". This is simply every element together in their purest form. It represents the chakra's place outside of the physical world. This chakra is completely spiritual; it is pure and unsullied by earthly faults. The color of the Ajna chakra is purple, though the quality of this energy point is not defined by its color, but rather by the luminance of that color. Purple represents the color of moonlight, the moon being a symbol of purity and spirituality.

The Ajna chakra is visualized as a transparent or lightly-colored lotus flower with two white petals that are placed horizontally on the left and right of the flower. These petals are believed to represent the two nadis (channels of psychic power), Ida and Pingala, which travel along the two sides of the body and meet the central channel, Sushumna nadi, at the third eye.

Once these three channels meet at the third eye, they then travel up to the crown chakra. The letter "ham" is found on the left petal and represents the deity Shiva, while on the right petal we will find the letter "ksham" which represents Shakti. In the center of the lotus is a depiction of Shakti sitting cross-legged with six faces and six arms, holding a skull, book, drum, and rosary. With their two free hands, Shakti is making gestures of giving gifts and dispelling fears.

As we have already seen, the Ajna is heavily linked to the deities Shakti and Shiva. These two are often seen as two sides of the same whole. In the context of this chakra, Shiva symbolizes consciousness and the masculine side of our minds, whilst Shakti symbolizes the activation of power and the feminine side of our minds. Shakti and Shiva work hand in hand to provide us with the power and knowledge to enlighten ourselves.

※

Crown Chakra

The final chakra on our journey to enlightenment is the crown chakra, or Sahasrara. Sahasrara translates to "thousand-petalled", this name stems from the thousands of different aspects of consciousness which this chakra is responsible for. As the name suggests, this chakra is found in the crown of our heads. It is said to be the most subtle and detached chakra in our bodies, only ever being utilized by those who have dedicated themselves fully to the pursuit of enlightenment. It is said that all the other chakras emanate from this one chakra.

When one is able to raise their Kundalini up through all of the chakras and into Sahasrara, they achieve Nirvikalpa Samadhi. This is a state of bliss and higher consciousness in which we are unwavered by whatever happens in the physical world. Those with the crown chakra opened can invoke a state of higher spirituality—one in which they are able to sever their ties to the earthly world and spiritually travel to other realms, see the past and future, and convene with spirits.

The Sahasrara is often associated with consciousness, connection to the spiritual world, liberation from earthly bonds, spiritual bliss, and higher wisdom or divine knowledge. This chakra is our primary link to the universe outside of our plane of existence. This is our source of divine energy and the consciousness that makes us human. This chakra is a cork in our bottle; it holds us in our physical body, often for our own good. But those who master themselves and the world around them are given the strength to remove that cork and venture outside of the world they knew before.

The crown chakra has no element per se but is rather represented by the universe and the divine light that fueled creation. This chakra is completely detached from our world, and therefore no earthly element could represent it. This chakra's link to the divine light is because the Sahasrara is the center of our consciousness, and our consciousness is what makes us. The colors of this chakra are pure white and gold. White represents the purity of mind and spirit needed to reach here, as well as the purity of the spiritual world. Gold symbolizes the divine light of creation and the power of the Kundalini that has awakened us.

The Sahasrara chakra is visualized as a thousand-petalled lotus. These petals are arranged in 20 rows each with 50 petals. The petals of this flower are multicolored and surround the center like a rainbow. The center of the flower is golden and within it is a shining triangle. This triangle can be both upward- and downward-facing. The Sahasrara chakra has no specific connections to any diety. This chakra is more representative of our journey to divinity. If a human is able to unlock it, they reach apotheosis, a level of divinity and spiritual strength that is celestial in its power.

SYMPTOMS OF CHAKRA IMBALANCE

Root Chakra

The root chakra is our source of emotional strength and is representative of the colon, bladder, legs, feet, and lower back. When we have a blockage or imbalance in our root chakra, we can see a variety of physical issues manifest such as incontinence, constipation, joint inflammation, gout, lower back pain, and stomach pain.

Because of the root chakra's importance in maintaining our emotional strength and mental wellbeing, it is crucial that we put time into making sure it is clear for our own mental health. Some mental symptoms of a blocked root chakra are anxiety related to basic needs, insecurity about money, feelings of being unsafe, abandonment anxiety, and codependency.

❦

Sacral Chakra

The sacral chakra is our source of love and pleasure and is representative of our reproductive organs, kidneys, and bladder. An imbalance in our sacral chakra can bring about many physical issues such as urinary/kidney infections, menstrual problems, gynecological cysts, impotence, infertility, and premature ejaculation.

The sacral chakra plays one of the most important roles for us in regards to mental health. Our ability to interact with people in meaningful ways and show love are reliant on the balance of this chakra. Therefore, blockage of it can lead to conditions like depression, insecurity, and jealousy. It can also result in self-esteem issues and self-isolation.

Solar Plexus Chakra

The solar plexus chakra is our source of energy and dynamism and represents our stomach, metabolism, and digestive system. An imbalance in it can cause a whole plethora of physical and psychological issues. Some of the physical issues that can indicate a blocked solar plexus chakra are stomach pains, indigestion, constipation, stomach ulcers, hypoglycemia, pre-diabetes, and weight gain.

The solar plexus is often seen as the source of our drive and inner strength. Because of this, a blocked solar plexus can lead to mental conditions and issues such as feelings of powerlessness, depression, low self-esteem, and lack of motivation. On the other hand, an overactive solar plexus chakra can lead to things like egomania, manic behavior, and hyperactivity.

Heart Chakra

The heart chakra is responsible for our love and connection to our spiritual side, and it also represents our heart and vascular system. An imbalance in this chakra can bring about plenty of emotional and relationship issues, as well as some physical discomforts. Some of the physical issues that can indicate an imbalanced heart chakra are upper back and shoulder pain, chest pain, heartburn, and high cholesterol.

The heart chakra is our source of love and is crucial to our relationships, and due to this, a blockage can be devastating to our personal lives. A blocked heart chakra can lead to plenty of emotional issues such as anxiety, fear of abandonment, feelings of loneliness, detachment, and irritability.

※

Throat Chakra

The throat chakra is responsible for our ability to communicate with others and make our thoughts a reality. An imbalance in it can bring about various physical and emotional symptoms due to the importance of this chakra in motivating us to be active and creative. Some of the physical symptoms of an imbalanced throat chakra are a sore throat, persistent coughing, vocal cord issues, thyroid dysfunctions, neck stiffness, jaw pain, and mouth ulcers.

The throat chakra is crucial to our personal and professional lives. It not only represents our ability to communicate, but our motivation to do things in life. Some symptoms of throat chakra imbalance are feelings of introversion, emotional instability, insecurity, and lack of motivation.

Third Eye Chakra

The third eye chakra is the driving force behind wisdom and intuition. Because of the important role it plays in our head, many of the issues caused by its imbalance are based around the brain. Some of the physical problems that may be caused by a blocked third eye chakra are as follows: headaches (particularly around the frontal lobe), ear infections, eye infections, inflammation around the eyes, and dizziness.

The third eye chakra has a key role in our mental wellbeing. This chakra plays a large part in our ability to problem-solve, learn, and interpret the world around us. Some psychological symptoms of an imbalance in this chakra are mental fog, difficulty in decision-making, inability to focus, over-analyzation, confusion, and lack of willpower.

Crown Chakra

Lastly is the crown chakra. It is the source of our spirituality and divine energy. Although this chakra is completely detached from our body, it can still have an effect on some areas of our brain, particularly the pineal gland and parietal lobe. Some of the physical issues that may be brought upon by an imbalance of this chakra are insomnia, lethargy, migraines, and mental fog.

The crown chakra is linked to our pineal gland, which controls our sleep cycles and states of consciousness. This means that imbalance in this area can cause sleep deficiencies which can lead to psychological issues and changes in one's personality if not dealt with. Some of these psychological issues may be cynicism, agitation, feelings of vulnerability, fear, and misanthropy.

WHAT CAUSES CHAKRA IMBALANCE?

In this section we're going to cover what the main causes of imbalance are for the seven major chakras. Some of them are simple to fix and others are more difficult, but all can be overcome with enough determination, meditation, and meaningful introspection.

Root Chakra

An imbalance or blockage of the root chakra can be brought upon by many things related to fear, trauma, laziness, and unhealthy eating. Fear and trauma are the two most common causes of a blocked root chakra. These tend to be deep-seeded issues that may take many sessions of meditation and introspection to overcome. Especially in cases of trauma, you may need the assistance of a professional psychologist. In the case of laziness, this can cause a chakra imbalance because of our root chakra's relation to Kundalini and the search for self-improvement. Lastly, unhealthy eating can also be a cause of chakra imbalance because of the root chakra's close association to the stomach. A bad diet or eating disorders can cause a blocked Muladhara chakra by interfering with the health of one's stomach and gut.

Sacral Chakra

The sacral chakra is one of the most commonly blocked or imbalanced chakras in today's high-stress, low-empathy world. Its blockage is often brought about by overindulgence in sexual desires, repression of sexual desires, codependence on a person or substance for pleasure, and emotional conflict. Both the overindulgence and lack of indulgence in sexual desires can cause a blockage of this chakra, because as with most things, we need to find balance. One should feel comfortable in their sexual freedom while still maintaining control over their instinctual desires.

Codependency is another major cause of blockage for this chakra. The sacral chakra is not only about loving others but also plays a big role in self-love. We should not need to rely on others to feel loved; rather, love should come from within primarily.

Lastly, emotional conflict can cause imbalance of this chakra. The sacral chakra is key in influencing our relationships with others, so emotional conflicts, especially ones with people we love, may impact the balance of this chakra.

Solar Plexus Chakra

The Manipura is one of the most important chakras for us to cultivate and work on. Without a balanced solar plexus, it may feel like we put in a lot more than we get out of life. Blockage of this chakra can be brought about by many factors, but mainly bad habits are to blame for imbalance here. As we've already mentioned, this chakra is our source of inner power and motivation; if we don't put that power to use, we could see an imbalance occur.

Idleness and indecisiveness are two of the primary causes of solar plexus chakra imbalance. An overflow of the power in this chakra can lead to either a blockage, which causes us to spiral further into inactivity, or an overload, which can cause us to become manic or hyperactive. Past trauma can also have a hand in causing imbalance in this chakra, and being spoiled and doted over as a child can lead to a shortage of willpower later in life. Conversely, early life neglect and oppression can lead to a restless spirit unable to focus itself on tasks. Either way, expert help may be needed to find closure and balance this chakra.

Heart Chakra

The Anahata chakra is definitely one that we want to put plenty of time and effort into keeping balanced. For all of our personal relationships to stay strong and well, we need to focus on maintaining its health. A blockage or imbalance of this chakra can be brought upon by many things, but it's usually caused by emotional trauma of some sort. Heartbreak and betrayal are the two most common forms of emotional trauma that affect it. These are things we must learn to come to terms with and move on from in order to restore balance.

A blockage can also occur in this chakra if we fail to share our love with others. Share love with our friends and family, commit acts of kindness toward strangers, and contribute to charities. By sharing our love with others, we allow for a healthy flow of energy in and out of our heart chakra.

※

Throat Chakra

The throat chakra is deceptively difficult to keep balanced. It requires us to be honest and authentic with everything we say and do in life. In today's world, white lies often seem like the lesser evil in social and professional matters. If we continue with this philosophy, we may find ourselves with a horribly imbalanced throat chakra. An imbalance of this chakra if most frequently caused by not living authentically and hiding our true selves from the world. It is responsible for much of our expression and social skills. If we withhold our true selves from the world, we stop this chakra from being able to fulfill its purpose.

A blockage of the throat chakra is also frequently caused by creative frustration. Failed previous attempts at expression can lead to negative thoughts which make us insecure and afraid to express ourselves further. One of the key methods for keeping this chakra in a balanced state is simply through consistently expressing one's personality and creative side.

Third Eye Chakra

Our third eye chakra is the source of much of our mental power and knowledge. When it suffers a blockage, it's usually due to a failure to exercise or an overuse of our intelligence. Both of these stem from the same basic cause of confusion and lack of clarity on our goals and desires. The third eye chakra needs constant stimulation, so we should never stop learning and training our minds. Enlightenment comes from wisdom and knowledge. But as with all things, we need balance. If we overwork our brains by overanalyzing simple thoughts and overwhelming ourselves with too much information all at once, we can also bring about a blockage.

Another potential blockage of the third eye chakra can come from not listening to our inner wisdom or "sixth sense". If we ignore the subtle signals that this chakra sends us, it may start to lose balance and potentially become blocked.

Crown Chakra

Finally, we have the crown chakra. This is a tough one to diagnose as it has few clear physical or psychological aspects. The crown chakra is the source of all chakras and, therefore, is directly affected when one of them falls into imbalance. Fear of death is one of the few psychological aspects of this chakra; whilst other energy points deal with fear as an emotion, the crown chakra deals specifically with our instinctual fear of death and our anxiety as to what lies beyond death. This form of existential fear and spiritual uncertainty can cause imbalance in the crown chakra.

Along with that, past traumas can also play a big role in unbalancing this chakra. Sudden losses of consciousness such as those caused by near death experiences and serious accidents can cause premature spiritual experiences in those who are not ready. This can cause the mind to actively avoid such occurrences in the future.

CHAPTER 2
BENEFITS OF CHAKRA HEALING

WHAT IS CHAKRA HEALING?

Chakra healing, or chakra balancing, is simply the process of making sure your chakras are functioning in ways that benefit you. There are many different stages of chakra health that one can reach. Some people put years of their lives into perfecting the health of chakras and opening them to their fullest. Most are content with having them in a balanced and healthy condition.

For those of us trying to balance our chakras in our day-to-day lives, we have a whole plethora of options available to us. From this point onward in the book, we will cover all the various conventional techniques for healing and balancing our chakras. Some require expert help, like reiki and massage, while others can be comfortably done every day regardless of work or studies.

But, before we get into the techniques needed to

heal our chakras, let's go over the reasons you want your chakras to be healed. It's all fair and well saying it's good for you, but it's understandable if you want some more details. Thus, below you will find details about the physical and mental benefits of healing and balancing each of the chakras.

THE BENEFITS OF HEALING YOUR CHAKRAS

Root Chakra

Healing the root chakra is the first step we should take toward attempting to heal and balance all of our chakras. As we have already established previously, this chakra is responsible for much of the lower body, and it's psychologically linked to our basic needs as humans. Healing it can be a fantastic quality of life improvement for anyone considering its important role in our day to day lives. By healing and balancing this chakra, we bring about feelings of comfort, security, and a general feeling of being at ease with the world around us.

Healing this chakra can also help to prevent various physical ailments such as constipation, joint pain, arthritis, stomach issues, and back pain. These physical ailments are easily treated and reduced by many of the healing techniques we will cover later in this book like meditation, massage, and healthy eating.

Sacral Chakra

As has already been mentioned, the sacral chakra is our source of love and pleasure. It helps us enjoy life and interact with other people in meaningful ways. The sacral chakra is heavily linked to our reproductive organs, our emotions concerning love and relationships, and our extraversion. Keeping this chakra balanced and healthy is crucial to maintaining a happy love life and an active social life. By healing it, we can ensure feelings of self-confidence, self-love, extraversion, and satisfaction.

We can help prevent or improve a multitude of physical conditions by healing this chakra. Some of the conditions we can easily help treat are impotence, premature ejaculation, gynecological cysts, and pelvic discomfort. All of these physical ailments can be treated by meditation, yoga, healthy eating, and massage.

Solar Plexus Chakra

When healing our chakras, we can never overlook the solar plexus. This chakra is so crucial to our general health and wellbeing that it should be a priority to keep it balanced at all times. Those of us who are hard-working professionals especially rely on this chakra as our energy source and the driving force behind our metabolism. Have you ever had one of *those* weeks? You know, the ones when you wake up every morning and feel completely exhausted and barely have the energy to make it to lunchtime. That is probably the result of an unbalanced solar plexus.

Having a balanced solar plexus can make a massive difference to our daily lives by giving us plenty of energy and feelings of power, optimism, and motivation. We can also alleviate a load of different physical problems by balancing this chakra. Issues like stomach ulcers, indigestion, high and low blood sugar, and other digestion-based ailments can easily be treated with healthy eating, aromatherapy, and yoga, among other things.

❂

Heart Chakra

Just like the solar plexus, the Anahata chakra is incredibly important and should be a definite focus for anyone looking to balance their chakras. Physically, it influences the health of our heart and circulatory system. Psychologically, this chakra is the source of our ability to feel and show love. Therefore, balancing it is crucial for our general health of both body and mind. I'm sure most of us have felt the heartbreak of a relationship ending. Well, that feeling can be reduced or even fully negated with a balanced heart chakra. By balancing it, we can improve our abilities to forgive, move on, and love again.

There are many physical ailments that a balanced heart chakra can help to treat and improve. Conditions like heartburn, high blood pressure, high cholesterol, poor circulation, heart palpitations, and shoulder/upper back pain.

Throat Chakra

Everyone has an artistic side. Some of us love to sing, others love to paint, and some play instruments. Whatever our chosen art is, we rely on this chakra to do it. The throat chakra is the source of our creativity and communication skills, so keeping it balanced is key for those of us who consider ourselves artists or just like to express ourselves freely. The positioning of this chakra is also important for our physical health and comfort. Our throat, lungs, and mouth all fall under it, and these regions are key areas to keep healthy. By balancing this chakra, we can improve our creativity, problem-solving skills, and our ability to communicate and persuade others.

There are a number of physical ailments that we may be able to help too. Conditions such as chest colds, mouth ulcers, thyroid issues, laryngitis, and jaw pain can all be helped by balancing this chakra.

Third Eye Chakra

If we've ever had one of those weeks where our luck just seems to be terrible, every gut decision we make backfires, or we feel like our judgment is wrong in everything, we probably have a blocked or unbalanced third eye chakra. As we've already covered, this chakra is our center of wisdom and knowledge. For all of us who are working and studying daily, it can be the difference between success and failure. This chakra doesn't have many effects on the physical body, but the negative ones that an imbalanced third eye can have are very painful and distracting.

Having a balanced third eye chakra can massively help with treating insomnia, nightmares, sleep-walking, and even mild depression. When it comes to physical issues, an imbalanced third eye chakra can be responsible for headaches, blocked sinuses, dizziness, exhaustion, and tired eyes. By balancing it, we can effectively lessen the impact of, or altogether treat, these illnesses.

Crown Chakra

Last of all comes the crown chakra. This is a difficult one to balance, but the benefits far outweigh the costs once you do. This chakra is inherently a purely psychological one. Its physical effects are few and are mainly felt through neurological disorders. By balancing it, not only are we helping to prevent all the symptoms of an unbalanced crown chakra, but we are helping to balance our whole being.

All the energy that every chakra needs to function comes from the crown chakra, thus a healthy crown chakra means a healthy flow of energy everywhere else. Balancing it results in having more clarity when choosing our direction in life, a better ability to stick to goals and targets, and a stronger connection to our spiritual side. On top of that, the neurological issues that we can avoid by working on this chakra include pineal gland disorders, migraines, depression, anxiety, and memory loss.

CHAPTER 3
MEDITATION AND CHAKRA HEALING TECHNIQUES

YOGA AND EXERCISE

Undoubtedly one of the best ways to balance and heal our chakras is through exercise and yoga. For thousands of years, Hindu, Buddhist, and Jain teachers have been stressing the importance of activity in opening one's chakras. This is especially true for our primarily physical chakras like the root, sacral, solar plexus, and heart chakras. These and the areas of the body around them need to be exercised.

The three big Indian religions all extensively teach about the holiness and sanctity of hard work and self-improvement. Although each chakra represents a different region of our physical form, our spirit as a whole benefits from self-care and a healthy body.

Root Chakra

The Muladhara chakra is balanced and healed through exercises and yoga that concern the lower body. In particular, exercises that strengthen the calf, quads, hamstrings, and glutes are fantastic for strengthening our grounding and improving our health. In terms of yoga poses, the root chakra has a few very useful ones that not only help channel spiritual energy up our spine, but help improve the blood flow and strength of muscles in the lower body.

The Ashwini mudra is one of the best known techniques for channeling Kundalini up the spine into the sacral chakra. In this yogic exercise, we want to seat ourselves comfortably on the floor, ideally in a lotus pose or easy pose. Once in position, we should take a few deep breaths, centering ourselves and controlling our breathing. Once we feel at peace we take another deep breath, hold it, contract the pelvic floor muscles, then relax them, and exhale. We should do up to five contractions, then take a break for a few breaths.

The Mahamudra is a common beginner pose that focuses on the root chakra. To do it, we want to start by sitting on the floor. One leg should be straight in front of us, the other is bent so that our foot is tucked under our buttocks. Take in a deep breath, and bend forward, exhaling. Grab hold of the foot of your straight leg with both hands. Lift your head and look forward. Hold this position for a few minutes, breathing normally, then switch legs.

Lastly comes the Manduki mudra (Bhadrasana).

This is a slightly more difficult pose meant for intermediate and experienced yoga practitioners. Our starting position is Vajrasana, a kneeling pose in which our heels are tucked under our buttocks. Next we spread our legs slightly and, exhaling, we bend forward and place our hands on the floor in front of us. Make sure the fingers point outward. Remain in the position and breath normally for a few minutes.

Sacral Chakra

The Svadhisthana chakra can be balanced and healed through exercises and yoga that focus on the pelvic, lower back, and lower abdominal areas. In particular, this includes exercises like kegels, bridges, crunches, and leg raises. In regards to yoga poses, the sacral chakra has a multitude of useful positions that both raise the spiritual strength of the chakra and help to increase blood flow and muscle health in the area.

The cobra pose, or Bhujangasana, is one yoga position that is very popular among yogis trying to balance their sacral chakra. One must start by laying on the ground on their abdomen. We then inhale and lift our upper half to a near-vertical position, pivoting on the Svadhisthana chakra. Once we are in the cobra pose, we exhale and hold the position for as long as comfortable. We then end the pose by exhaling as we slowly lower ourselves to the starting position.

Repeat this pose up to three times before taking a break.

The bridge pose, or Setuasana, is another very popular pose for this chakra. This pose is fantastic for relieving lower back pain and building strength in that muscle area. We start by sitting upright with legs straight in front of us. We concentrate on the sacral chakra and place our hands on the floor behind our body with fingers pointing backward. Then, while inhaling, we lift our upper body and pelvic area. Our hands should support our weight. Relax the neck and let the head hang back. Breathe normally and remain in this position as long as possible before exhaling and slowly returning to the starting position.

The Yoga Mudra is a mudra focused on helping increase the flow of energy into the sacral chakra and promoting the movement of Kundalini. This mudra starts in the Vajrasana position, kneeling with your feet tucked under your buttocks and your hands on your lap. Relax the whole body and close the eyes. Then, take in a deep breath and raise your arms above your head. Now exhale and keep the back straight as you slowly bend forward until your forehead touches the floor. Rest your arms beside your body with the palms facing upward. Relax in this position and breath normally for as long as you wish. Then inhale and bring the body back upright with arms raised. Lastly, exhale and return to the starting position.

Solar Plexus Chakra

The solar plexus, or Manipura, can be healed and empowered through various yoga poses and exercises that focus on the abdominal muscles and the back. In regards to exercises, there are quite a few easy-to-do and very effective exercises for this chakra. Some of those exercises include sit-ups, planking, back extensions, leg raises, and cat curls. When it comes to yoga poses, the solar plexus has a bunch of incredibly effective poses that help to stimulate your central organs, strengthen your core, and assist the channeling of vital life force energy around your body.

The full boat pose, or Paripurna Navasana, is a favorite among yogis looking to empower their core muscles and strengthen their focus. To achieve this pose, you must start in an upright, seated position with your legs straight and arms at your side. This position is known as the staff pose. You engage the muscles along your core and spine to keep your posture completely erect. You then move your shoulder blades up and back and push out your chest. Your upper body and lower body should now form a 90-degree angle at your hips.

Now you tilt your back slightly and take your weight onto your sitting bones, keeping your back engaged so you don't hunch. Next, raise your legs, regaining the 90-degree angle you had. Lastly, raise your arms and keep them parallel with the floor, forming a bridge between your torso and legs. Hold this position for as long as possible, and then repeat the instructions in reverse, coming back to your seated position.

The firefly pose, or Tittibhasana, is an intermediate-to-advanced yoga pose which focuses on improving balance, core strength, and arm strength. In order to perform this pose, you must start in a low squat with your feet shoulder-distance apart and your pelvis at knee-height. Next take your left hand and place it on the floor next to your left foot, fingers pointing forward. Do the same for your right-hand side. Very slowly, rock back and feel your center of gravity tilt. Your hands should now be taking most of the weight of our body. Inhale as you lift your legs off the floor and take all of your weight onto your hands. Your pelvis should be high so that your legs are parallel to the floor at this point. Without tensing your neck, look forward and breathe slowly for 15 seconds or longer if possible. Finally, with an exhale, you can lower your legs to the floor and rest.

Lastly, we have the Bharadvaja's twist, or Bharadvajasana. This is a relatively simple, seated yoga pose that helps to activate energy flow up the spine, strengthen the back, and encourage better posture. The first step of this pose starts with the same seated position as the Paripurna Navasana, with the legs straight and torso upright. Imagine a central axis running along your spine, from your pelvic floor to your crown. Your back should at all times be as straight as possible; this axis should never bend or curve.

Keeping this in mind, shift your weight onto your

right hip, and swing your legs to the left. Your left leg should rest under your left buttock. Your right leg should be resting on your left thigh. Recenter your balance back onto both hips. Now, you must twist your body, using the abdominal muscles, to the right. Lastly, place your right hand onto your left knee, and wrap your left arm around your back. Hold this position for up to 10 breaths, and then release back into the original seated position. Repeat this, mirroring your actions on the other side.

Heart Chakra

The heart chakra is actually one of the easier chakras to balance and strengthen through exercise and yoga. It focuses on the chest, heart, circulatory system, and blood. Exercises for this chakra are pretty straightforward. The cardiovascular system is greatly benefited by cardio like running, cycling, rowing, and swimming. Along with that, you can strengthen the muscles of the chest through push-ups, bench presses, and butterfly chest presses. When it comes to yoga, there are plenty of poses that focus on building stamina, aiding blood flow, lowering blood pressure, and helping the flow of energy out of the heart chakra.

The first heart chakra pose we will explore is the cow face pose, or Gomukhasana. In order to achieve this, you must start in the staff position with your legs straight ahead of you and torso upright. Continuing, you need to bend your knees and place your feet onto the ground. Then slide your left foot under your right knee, and cross over your right knee to the left. You want your two knees to be stacked on top of each other with your feet next to your hips. Once your legs are in position, rest evenly on your sitting bones. Next, take your right arm and reach it straight out to your right, parallel to the floor. Turn the arm inwardly, first with your thumb pointing to the floor, then again with your thumb pointing behind you with the palm toward the ceiling. While exhaling, swing the arm behind and into the hollow of your back.

With your arm parallel to your waist, roll your shoulder back and work your forearm up until it is in line with your spine. The back of your hand should now be resting between our shoulder blades. Next, take your left arm and stretch it out toward the wall in front of you, palm-side up. Continue this movement by lifting this arm up to the ceiling, and in one fluid movement, bend at the elbow and reach down behind you to meet the other hand. Attempt to interlock the fingers of both hands and hold that position for a minute, maintaining normal breathing. Repeat the process on the opposite side.

The second yoga pose that we will look at is the eagle pose, or Garudasana. To start, stand upright with arms at your side; this is called Tadasana, or mountain pose. Continue by bending your knees slightly and lifting your left foot up. Cross your left leg over your right and hook your left foot behind your lower right calf. Your next move is to raise your arms up parallel to the floor. Turn them palm-side up and cross them over at the elbow.

Continuing this movement, bend your arms at the elbow and rest your left arm in the crook of your right elbow. The backs of your hands should be facing each other now, and your fingers should be pointing at the ceiling. Lastly, you want to twist your right hand to the right and left hand to the left; this should cause your palms to both face each other. Hold this position for up to 30 seconds, unwind, and repeat for the opposite side.

Our last heart chakra pose is the camel pose, or Ustrasana. You begin this pose by kneeling on the floor. Your thighs and torso should be vertical. Keeping your knees hip-distance apart, you want to press the top of your feet down onto the floor and straighten your ankles. Next bring your palms together in front of your chest and drop your chin down into the chest. Take a deep breath, and push your palms out so that they face in front of you. With the following exhalation, move your hands around your body and down to your heels. Then press upward with the spine, and puff out your chest as far as you can before relaxing your neck and letting your head hang back. Hold this position for 10 breaths, and then return to the kneeling pose.

Throat Chakra

The throat chakra is the first of the three spiritual chakras. This is the point where physical exercise becomes less important; spiritual exercise is more instrumental in developing this chakra. There are plenty of yoga poses that are still very effective at helping to develop, heal, and open up this chakra despite its ethereal nature. In regards to physical exercise, you can still rely on neck, shoulder and upper back exercises to help activate and balance it. Exercises like neck rotations, shoulder rolls, chair rotations, thoracic extensions, and dumbbell rows are all fantastic for building strength and flexibility in the region of the throat chakra. For yoga, there are plenty of poses that focus around stretching and loosening up the throat and neck, as well as help with the expression of energy from the throat chakra.

The first pose we are looking at is the fish pose, or Matsyasana. This is a very simple, yet effective pose for opening up the throat chakra. You start with your back to the floor, knees bent and feet planted flat on the ground. Pressing down with your feet, lift your hips off the ground. You can then proceed to place your hands on the floor with your palms down, and then slide your hands under your hips.

At this point, your buttocks should be resting on your hands. Then, with one foot at a time, you lower and straighten your legs. You should try to stretch your big toes and flatten your feet as far as possible. Going back to your torso, you should now puff out your chest and engage your spine. Be sure to engage only the spine and not the neck. Your neck and head should be relaxed and hanging. Hold this pose for 10 breaths, and then return to your starting position.

Our next throat chakra pose is the supported shoulderstand, or Salamba Sarvangasana. This is an intermediate pose that is especially good at unblocking and activating the throat chakra. To start, you need two or more yoga mats or thick blankets folded into one by two foot rectangles. Stack these rectangles on top of each other, and then lie on them. Be sure that when you lie on these mats, your shoulders are on the mat but your head is on the floor.

Once comfortable, you can lay your arms beside your torso, bend your knees up, and lay your feet flat onto the floor. Exhaling, try to press your feet and arms into the floor, lifting your body up. Continue to slowly lift yourself up, pushing the pelvis away from the floor and using your arms to support you by bringing them out to your sides and in line with your shoulders. Moving your arms further, you should bend your elbows, rest your upper arms on the mat, and bring your hands up to your back.

Now, raise your pelvis over your shoulders so that your torso is nearly perpendicular to the floor. Next, you can inhale and lift your legs up toward the ceiling, starting with your bent knees, then extending further to include your whole legs. Finally, relax the neck and throat, tense the shoulders, and push the chin outward. Your forehead should be parallel to the floor, and your shoulders should be holding a majority of your weight. Start by holding this pose for only 30 seconds, and gradually add more time as it becomes easier and more comfortable.

Lastly is the child's pose, or Balasana. The first step is to kneel on the floor and spread your knees hip-width apart. You will then exhale and lay your torso down onto your thighs, arch your back slightly so that there is no pressure on your spine, and extend your neck out, bringing your forehead parallel to the floor. Continue by laying your hands on the floor, palm-side down, out in front of your body. Your shoulders should be relaxed and your arms should hang to the floor. Hold this pose for a few minutes while maintaining normal breathing.

Third Eye Chakra

The third eye chakra is a primarily mental chakra. As such, normal physical exercises won't do too much to help heal or strengthen this chakra. However, mental exercises are incredibly effective in keeping the mind healthy and helping this chakra to open up. Doing a few daily exercises such as a jigsaw puzzle, crossword, sudoku, practicing an instrument, learning a language, or doing a memory training exercise can all provide massive benefits toward healing and strengthening this chakra. In regards to yoga poses, we are mainly going to be focusing on resting poses, which encourage relaxation and better blood flow to the brain.

First off is the downward-facing dog pose, or

Adho Mukha Svanasana. This is one of the most well-known poses in the practice of yoga. The position we will take up here is perfect for increasing blood and energy flow to the brain. Starting off, you position yourself on your hands and knees. You need your wrists to be in line with your shoulders and your knees to be in line with your hips. In one swift movement, tense your legs, curl your toes under your feet, and lift your legs and hips up into a straightened position. You should try to engage your quads and avoid locking your knees.

Next, you can extend your arms and lift your torso up with your quads carrying most of your weight. Again, make sure not to lock your elbows. Hold this position for 10 breaths or as long as you are comfortable. Once done, you can exhale and bend your knees to release the pose and come back down into your starting position.

The next pose is the hero pose, or Virasana. This one is a simple seated resting pose that is often used as an alternative to the lotus pose. Although this is one of the least physically intensive poses in yoga, it is an incredibly powerful position for meditation. You will start by positioning yourself on your knees. Your thighs should be perpendicular to the floor, and your knees should be touching. Following that, you will slide your feet apart slightly past your hips, and angle your big toes slightly inward.

Next, exhale and sit down between your feet. If your buttocks is not resting on the floor, feel free to use a book or folded mat to support it. Next you will proceed to lay your hands palm-side down on your kneecaps, firm your shoulders, and puff out your chest. Be sure to keep good back posture. Maintain this pose with normal breathing for as long as comfortable. Also, feel free to try meditating in this pose once comfortable.

Our last third eye chakra pose is the big toe pose, or Padangusthasana. This position is incredibly effective at directing energy down the spine and into the third eye. In order to achieve this pose, you must start in a standing position. Your feet must be roughly six inches apart, and your legs should be completely straight without locked knees. Proceed to bend over, bending the knees slightly if needed, and hook your index and middle fingers into the space between your big and second toes. Next, with a deep breath in, you will lift our upper body as if you were going to stand again, straightening your arms. As you exhale, you will flex and release your glutes while relaxing your lower back.

Following that, you should push out your chest and straighten your neck, taking care to not compress your neck and put pressure on it. Take another few deep breaths, and with each inhale, you should try to lift your torso, flex your quads, and flex your glutes. Finally, stretch forward into a comfortable bend, and hold the position for one minute, breathing normally. Afterwards, you can release your toes, bring your hands to your hips, and in one motion, swing your torso and head back up in a controlled manner.

Crown Chakra

The crown chakra is a completely spiritual chakra, and for this reason, no exercises of a mental or physical nature are going to affect it directly. The only way for us to heal and strengthen this chakra is through spiritual exercises, such as meditation, fasting, abstinence, crystal healing, and aligning all of the other chakras.

Our first crown chakra position is the plow pose, or Halasana. This is a relatively difficult position but works wonders for healing and empowering the crown chakra. The plow pose is an extension of the supported shoulderstand, which is the starting point. Once in the supported shoulderstand position, you exhale and bend forward from the hips, bringing your legs above and over your head. You should try to keep your torso as vertical as possible and ensure that your legs are straight at all times.

With your toes touching the floor, you should tense your thighs and tailbone while flexing your pelvic floor. Your arms can either stay in the supported shoulderstand position of supporting your back, or if more comfortable, you can lower your arms and stretch them out behind you. Continue to flex the pelvic floor and take your weight on your thighs. Hold this pose for up to five minutes. To exit this position, simply lift your legs back into the supported shoulderstand and roll down onto your back.

Secondly, we have the seated forward bend, or Paschimottanasana. This pose is a relaxed resting pose and serves to help relax our mind, body, and spirit. To start out, you want to sit on the floor with your buttocks on a folded mat and your legs directly out in front of you. Following that, you can shift your weight onto your left buttock and stretch your right leg completely. Then you will switch sides and do the same for your left leg. Next, place your palms onto the floor next to your hips, and push your chest out toward the ceiling. You need to then inhale and lean forward from your hips. If possible, reach for the sides of your feet and hold them with your hands as you bend forward.

Once comfortable, you continue the forward bend by bringing your belly down onto your thighs, then your ribs, and finally your head near your feet. Always try to keep good posture and avoid bending your elbows. With each breath, flex the muscles of your torso and increase the forward bend. By doing this, you gradually increase your flexibility and lengthen your reach further. Stay in this pose for up to three minutes. To return to normal, you can gradually lift your torso away from your thighs and relax your arms.

The final pose for the crown chakra is the reclining bound angle pose, or Supta Baddha Konasana. This position is an extension of Baddha Konasana, a simple seated pose in which you sit upright with the bottoms of the feet touching. To perform this pose, you start in Baddha Konasana.

Your first move is to exhale and recline your lower back toward the floor, leaning on your hands. Then lower yourself further so that now your forearms are bearing your weight. Using your hands, you support your lower back as you bring your torso all the way down onto the floor.

Next, you will position your arms at a 45-degree angle from your upper body, palms up and relaxed. To stretch your pelvis, you need to engage the muscles in your groin and flex them; this will relax your glutes and improve the stretch you receive from this pose. You must be careful to not press your knees down into the floor, as it can actually lessen the effect desired from this position. Rather than letting your knees drift toward the ceiling, let them hang in the air weightlessly.

Stay in this pose for one minute at the beginning, but feel free to increase the duration once you are more comfortable. To come out of this pose, you will use your hands to push your legs together. Then, you can roll to one side and push yourself up onto your hands and knees.

MEDITATION

Meditation is arguably the most ancient and sacred form of spiritual empowerment. Nearly every religion from Buddhism and early Abrahamic religions, to Native American religions and everything in between has used meditation as a way of aligning oneself and reaching higher planes of consciousness. Meditation is one of the longest studied and practiced skills in human history. Intellectuals throughout time have explored the intricacies of this practice. But those of you who are inexperienced in the matter may wonder what meditation actually is.

Well, meditation is simply a deeper form of concentration. That is what we hope to achieve whenever we meditate. Every time we close our eyes, control our breathing, and chant a mantra, we are trying to reach that deeper level of focus, awareness, and concentration. It sounds a lot more simple than it is because, in truth, meditation is a skill that has many levels to it. Almost anyone can sit in a quiet room and meditate to calm themselves, but not everyone can heighten their senses, achieve emotional clarity, or heal their chakras.

These are only some of the things which will come with practicing meditation. One of the key goals of any meditator is to reach a stage of total self-awareness. After achieving complete calm and concentration, we can perceive ourselves within ourselves. In other words, we are able to look at ourselves from an outside perspective—one free of bias or ego. From this position, it is possible to make the best decisions for ourselves, notice our errors, and appreciate our successes.

Meditation has been scientifically observed to have multiple benefits for our physical and mental wellbeing. Regular meditation may significantly lower feelings of stress, depression, anxiety, and chronic pain. Meditation has also been shown to lower blood pressure, increase attention span, and improve quality of sleep. It results in all of these benefits with no known downsides aside from the 30 minutes you need to take out of your day to perform it.

As with yoga, meditation is something that is best taught by a master rather than learned on one's own. Luckily, guided meditations are incredibly easy to come across, and it's almost guaranteed that whatever we may need from a guided meditation is already available somewhere online. In the sections below, we will go over the meditations for each chakra, what we hope to focus on, the best places to meditate, and the goals of each meditation.

Preparations

Before we cover the intricacies of meditating on each chakra, let's go over the key areas of any meditation. These are the initial steps and tips to follow while starting a form of meditative practice. Although there are hundreds of different types of meditation, they all have the same core concepts of breathing control and relaxation.

- **Position yourself comfortably.** Seat yourself on the floor, a mat, or a chair in an upright position. Make sure your spine is straight and that you are at a comfortable temperature.
- **Slow your breathing.** Typically we want to keep a pattern of breathing in for three to five seconds, holding the breath in our lungs for three to five seconds, and then exhaling fully for three to five seconds. Find the rhythm you're most comfortable with and stick with it.
- **Relax your muscles.** Once you fall into a comfortable breathing rhythm, you will start to feel your muscles relax. Ignore the temptation to move fingers, flex muscles, or scratch your nose. If you do need to move, make sure that it is in slow and fluid movements.
- **Close your eyes.** Your eyes should be naturally closing themselves at this point. It is possible that your eyelids will be feeling very heavy, and your eyes may even lose focus as you drift into an ultra-relaxed state.
- **Clear your mind.** Some of us have an easier time clearing our mind than others. Personally, I have an overly active

imagination, so I find it hard to completely empty all my thoughts from my head at times. I find it often just takes time to learn how to do this. You may need a few more minutes than you expected, but just try your best to persevere and stick with it. As long as you keep focusing on your breathing, your mind will declutter itself naturally.
- **Don't force it.** This is arguably the most important point to take note of for anyone new to meditation. Do not force any stage of the process. Focus on your breathing, and with time, everything will come naturally to you.

Root Chakra

The root chakra is the first chakra that we will look to heal and strengthen. Meditation on this chakra usually involves focusing on your basic needs and insecurities. Your primary goal when meditating on this energy point is grounding. You are stripping away your material worries and reminding yourself of your connection to the earth. If you often feel worried about your needs and wants in life, then meditating frequently on this chakra may bring you peace.

Below, we will cover some of the common themes and ideas behind root chakra meditations.

- **Meditate outside**: The root chakra is your grounding point to the world that surrounds you. By meditating outside, on the ground, and in nature, you can absorb the energy around your body which is related to this chakra. Meditating on dirt, rock, or at least with a pot of soil next to you will massively strengthen the connection you make with the earth around you.
- **Focus on the position of this chakra**: The root chakra is located at the base of your spine. Try to think of it as a well that you need to dip a bucket into in order to get spiritual energy from it. Focus on channeling energy from the root chakra up your spine. Imagine a trickle at first that with every breath grows until it eventually becomes a torrent.
- **Visualize the color**: The color of this chakra is a deep, earthy red, the color of hot lava, a beautiful lotus flower, and of soft pottery clay. Imagine that color radiating from the base of your spine, up into your torso, and down into your legs. The color of this energy point is warm and comforting. If you feel anxious outside of meditation, try to imagine that same red glow spreading through your body.
- **Use the mantra**: The mantra that corresponds to this chakra is "Lam"

(pronounced L-ahm). Once deep into your meditation, using a clear mind, formulate the Lam mantra. You will want to picture the letters of the mantra entering your mind as you say them. Focus completely on the word as you slowly chant it out loud in time with your breathing.

Sacral Chakra

The second chakra that we will look to meditate on, the sacral chakra, is one we will very commonly feel is locked. To heal and unblock this chakra, you will find yourself focusing on your creativity, sexuality, and self-image. Your primary goal when meditating on the sacral chakra is to build a better sense of self-worth, creative freedom, and self-confidence. If you often feel insecure, struggle with creativity, or feel guilty about sexual emotions, then meditating frequently on this chakra is something you need to do.

Below, you will find some of the common themes behind meditating on the sacral chakra.

- **Meditate near water**: Water is the element of this chakra as it reflects the fluid and flowing nature of this chakra's energy. Try to meditate near water, whether that be the ocean, a lake, a pool, or even a bowl filled with water. Great rivers are massive sources of sacral chakra energy and thus make the best meditation locations for this chakra.

- **Focus on the position of this chakra**: The sacral chakra is located between the navel and sexual organs. The power from this chakra flows down into the sexual organs and up into the solar plexus. Try to imagine that flow of energy in both directions when meditating on this energy point.
- **Visualize the color**: The color of this chakra is a bright, radiant orange. It is the shade of a juicy orange or a perfectly ripened pumpkin. Picture this refreshing and exciting color in your mind whenever you need to focus on this energy point.
- **Use the mantra**: The mantra of this chakra is "Vam" (pronounced V-ahm). Once you're into a meditative state and are successfully visualizing the movement of this chakra's energy, try repeating the mantra. Focus on it completely, and imagine it aiding the flow of energy from this energy point.

Solar Plexus Chakra

Our third chakra on the journey up the spine, the solar plexus, is another energy point that is very commonly in some stage of imbalance. Often people who work in high stress environments and don't take care to eat properly will suffer blockages here the most.

In order to heal and unblock this chakra, we will be focusing on willpower, drive to work, and feelings of pride and achievement. Your goals when working on this chakra are to achieve a more rigid sense of self-discipline, a greater drive to work toward things, and a feeling of pride in who you are and what you have accomplished. If you often suffer from feelings of helplessness, lack of motivation, or a lack of self-respect, then it may be good for you to spend some time working on this energy point.

- **Meditate near fire**: The solar plexus is the source of our inner fire, and therefore, meditating near fires is a fantastic way of recharging and rebalancing this chakra. That fire can be anything from a burning candle to a simple campfire or raging bonfire. As long as you have your fire in a safe place, it will work for this meditation.
- **Focus on the position of this chakra:** This chakra is found in the middle of the torso, above the navel and below the lungs. This chakra radiates energy all around the body from this central position. Imagine a network of bright yellow veins networking out from the center of your body into the extremities.

- **Visualize the color**: The color of this chakra is yellow which represents the brilliant vibrancy of the energy that it produces. Think of a ripe lemon or a brilliant ray of sunlight; that is the color you should visualize if you ever need to connect yourself to this chakra.
- **Use the mantra**: The mantra of the solar plexus chakra is "Ram" (pronounced R-ahm). Whenever you meditate on this energy point, repeat this mantra in long, elongated syllables with every exhale. By doing this, you will be mimicking the flow of energy out of your solar plexus.

Heart Chakra

The heart chakra is the halfway point toward enlightenment. The chakra is the middle ground between the physical and spiritual, which means it can be pretty temperamental and complicated at times. This chakra is most commonly upset by failure in things that mean a lot to us, whether that be relationships, work, or personal goals. In order to heal and balance this energy point, you will be focusing your meditations on your ability to show love, receive love, and forgive others and yourself. Your goals with heart chakra meditation are to strengthen your emotional strength, improve your ability to love, and heal any feelings of hurt or betrayal.

If you often experience feelings of being unloved, feelings of being distant from others, and feelings of abandonment, then meditation on the heart chakra is definitely needed.

- **Meditate in nature**: The heart chakra is intrinsically linked to nature. In order for us to thrive as humans, we need to show love to the world around us, and that world is the nature that we see everyday. Our heart is also the part of our body that we have to keep healthy above all others. Nature represents health; where plants and animals are healthy, everything else is healthy too. Try to meditate surrounded by plants, in grass, or even with your pets (if they aren't too distracting).
- **Focus on your heartbeat**: This chakra is located in the center of your chest but it directly channels energy through the heart. Focusing on your heartbeat during meditation can bring you to a deeper state of relaxation and closeness to this chakra. Just imagine, with every beat, your love for the world around you grows, and with it your health.
- **Visualize the color**: The color of this chakra is the shade of healthy nature: green. Think of a lush green pasture or a strong vine growing up a temple wall. Visualizing this color pumping through

your veins and enveloping you while you meditate is a powerful way of boosting the energy of this chakra.
- **Use the mantra**: Lastly, make use of this chakra's mantra, "Yam" (pronounced Y-ahm). Repeat this mantra in times of emotional uncertainty. Use long elongated syllables and sync it to your breathing for the best results.

Throat Chakra

The throat chakra is the first of our spiritual chakras, and therefore, meditation is particularly effective in helping to heal and balance this energy point. Being your center for expression, this chakra is one that can be upset on a daily basis by any number of factors. Typically, you may see imbalances being caused if you don't voice your concerns or opinions, don't express yourself, or even try to suppress others from expressing themselves.

Your goals when meditating on this chakra are to build confidence in speaking and expression, help clear your mind to make room for creative thoughts, and create a more open-minded view of others' expressions. If you have feelings of shame about your art, a mind cluttered by ideas, or an anxiety when it comes to speaking to others, then you need to work on the throat chakra.

- **Meditate with ambient noise**: This chakra is represented by sound in our world, specifically sounds of expression like chants, prayers, music, speeches, poetry, or even an audiobook. These are all sounds of expression that will nourish this chakra and perhaps provide you with the inspiration you need. So next time you plan to meditate on this chakra, play some calm ambient music, rhythmic drums, quiet poetry, or even a soft spoken audiobook in the background.
- **Focus on sounds**: Continuing from the last point, now that you have something playing in the background, try to focus on it. This may seem difficult at first, but focusing on a specific beat, sound, or frequency can help you easily fall into a deep trance. Meditating in this manner also allows you to directly connect with the primary source of energy for this chakra, making it a very efficient way of empowering it.
- **Visualize the color**: Violet and deep blue are the key colors that represent this chakra. These are the colors of the night sky and heavily-burdened storm clouds. Picture a calming rain or a violet sunset while meditating on this chakra. These scenes are both cool and relaxing yet warming and active at the same time.

- **Use the mantra**: Finally, we want to make use of this chakra's mantra, "Ham" (pronounced H-ahm). This mantra in particular resonates and vibrates strongly in the throat when chanted, which can be therapeutic for those of you who suffer from a sore throat.

Third Eye Chakra

The third eye chakra is the penultimate chakra in this journey to enlightenment. Meditation on this energy point is a key part in balancing it, because doing so helps to clear and calm the areas of the mind that this chakra influences most. You will typically see imbalances in the third eye chakra caused by a lack of clarity in your goals, ignoring your intuition, and refusing divine guidance.

Your goals when meditating on this chakra are to bring clarity to your mind, open yourself up to wisdom, and allow for divine guidance to positively influence you. If you have feelings of confusion in life, a feeling of being without purpose, and feelings of disconnection from your inner wisdom, then you need to spend time working on the third eye chakra.

- **Meditate in a place with multiple elements**: This chakra is represented by the supreme element, a combination of all elements in one. Now, it may be hard to find all elements in one place, but you can at least meditate near a few that will definitely have a beneficial impact. Another option is to set up an altar with a bowl of water, a bowl of soil, a healthy plant, and some ambient noises.

- **Focus on space**: This chakra is associated with space—with the emptiness and calm of the void. If you clear your mind and free your consciousness, you can gain access to so much room for thought, inspiration, and deliberation. Meditating in this manner allows you to make direct contact to the realm from which divine wisdom flows.
- **Visualize the color**: The color of this chakra is purple, between the vibrancy of lavender and the darkness of distant space. When meditating on this energy point, try to picture a warm, purple void through which you are drifting. Allow it to encircle and envelope you.
- **Use the mantra**: This mantra has two parts. The first is "Ksham" (pronounced Sh-ahm), and the second and most well-known is "Om". Yes, this is the same Om that people say to imitate Buddhist monks. It is the basic sound of the universe and is believed to contain all other sounds.

Crown Chakra

Last of all, the crown chakra is the source of all our other chakras. This hub needs regular maintenance and attention, otherwise everything could fall into imbalance. This energy point can be sent into imbalance by a number of things, including other chakras being severely thrown off track, spiritual ignorance, and a lack of divine energy finding its way into your body. Your goals when meditating on this chakra are finding inner peace, opening yourself up to divine energy, and searching for spiritual enlightenment.

Feelings of spiritual doubt, a disconnect from the world, and apathy may be caused by issues relating to this chakra and should be dealt with right away with meditation and other healing techniques.

- **Meditate in the midday sun**: The crown chakra is not associated with any earthly element but rather with the divine light and the greater universe. In order to tap into this source of energy and connect to this chakra in a deeper way, you can meditate in the midday sun. The sun you feel in the middle of the day is not only the hottest and purest, but it shines directly down onto the crown of your head.
- **Focus on the divine**: When meditating on this chakra, try to focus on the divine. Picture your gods or spirits—picture the creation of the universe and the brilliance

of the sun shining light down onto the earth. Meditating on these images helps your crown chakra to open and, in turn, it opens you up to divine wisdom.
- **Visualize the color**: The colors of this chakra are gold and white. When you meditate on this chakra, make sure to incorporate these divine colors into your clothing, surroundings, and thoughts.
- **Use the mantra**: Finally, the mantra of this chakra is the universal sound of "Om". However, complete silence is also a powerful catalyst for this chakra. After all, the universe is silent and so should be our minds when meditating on this chakra.

VISUALIZATION

Visualization is a very simple yet effective technique for improving your mental and physical well-being. The name is rather self-explanatory; we visualize what we want, and through the focused power of our chakras, we can make it so. Now, visualization isn't going to make a sports car appear in front of you, and it definitely won't turn your home into a mansion, but it can heal your chakras and help you make changes to yourself that you truly desire.

Visualization is most powerful during moments of calm and meditation. The process is rather simple. You get comfortable, bring yourself into a state of meditation, and then visualize the changes you want to make while maintaining a state of total calm. The types of changes you can bring about are nearly endless, but most revolve around the way you perceive yourself and the world around you.

If you feel symptoms of a blockage in your solar plexus, visualization may be an efficient way of clearing it away by focusing on the color, mantra, and element of the chakra. Along with focusing directly on chakras, you can also direct your attention to the causes of chakra imbalance themselves. Let's say, for example, that you are insecure about your weight, and it is impacting your ability to love yourself. This is causing a blockage in your heart chakra. By visualizing yourself loving yourself and others loving you as you are, you can overcome those insecurities.

Visualizing goals is another way to utilize this

mindfulness technique. Our brains certainly are not perfect machines. In fact, they can be fooled pretty easily. We can use that to our advantage, however, by visualizing our goals. While doing so, you can trick your brain into thinking that those goals have already been achieved. Although you know they haven't been, a part of your brain will feel more confident and capable of achieving those goals.

This is all due to a phenomenon called neuroplasticity. The images that we put in our brain evoke certain feelings, whether those images are actually real or not. These feelings can come back into use whenever we are reminded of those images. Thus, we can program ourselves to feel more confident when we are approached with certain situations.

AFFIRMATIONS

Affirmations are a key part of healing our chakras. These are truths that we tell ourselves to counteract the lies that we believe about ourselves. When our chakras are unbalanced, we may feel insecure, uncomfortable, and unhappy about aspects of our lives and ourselves. In order to balance and heal those chakras we need to acknowledge and accept that those insecurities are false and do nothing but poison our self-image. Through affirmations, we condition ourselves to think positively and to reject insecure thoughts. Each chakra has different affirmations that target certain aspects associated with those areas of our body and mind.

Affirmations can be used in multiple ways but the two most common are through meditation and daily repetition. When using affirmations in meditation, we wait until we are in a deep meditative state, and then we visualize the affirmations we need to hear entering into our mind one by one. We focus on every word and imprint each onto our consciousness. By repeating these affirmations to ourselves in this heightened state of awareness, we nullify our own mind's ability to contradict us. In our state of deep meditation, our mind is only open to truths, so every affirmation will be taken into our mind as the whole truths that they are.

When using affirmations in daily repetition, the name is pretty self-explanatory. The idea is that we set up multiple times throughout the day where we repeat a few affirmations to ourselves. These affirmations can be targeting a specific chakra, or they can be targeted toward our whole being in general. Most of the time, we tend to do these repetitions around three times a day—after waking, at the middle of our waking hours, and before we sleep. However, we can actually repeat these affirmations whenever we feel we need them. If you happen to be in a situation that makes you feel insecure, repeat the necessary affirmations to yourself and take in some deep, meditative breaths.

Root Chakra

For the root chakra, our affirmations primarily revolve around safety, security, and stability. This energy point is most commonly associated with being the spiritual base and the source of our connection to the world around us. Therefore, any affirmations you read, say, and create will have some link toward reassuring the support you need and get from the world around you.

Some affirmations for the root chakra are as follows:

- "I will be safe and secure wherever I am."
- "I am safe and content in my home."
- "My safety needs will always be fulfilled by the earth."
- "At this moment, I am grounded, stable, and at peace."

- "I am grounded to the earth, and I am supported by the universe."
- "I am deserving of support whenever I need it."
- "I will receive support whenever I need it."
- "I have a strong body, a healthy mind, and a balanced spirit."
- "The world will always support me and provide for me."
- "My root chakra is opening, and I feel myself becoming balanced."
- "I feel the energy of the earth spread through my body."

Sacral Chakra

For the sacral chakra, our affirmations are primarily based on expression, creativity, and self-love. This chakra is our source of sensual energy, self-confidence, and creativity. This means that any affirmations you use for this chakra will be very personal and intimate in nature. These affirmations may be hard to say at first because of this very personal nature, but they are important for us to hear.

- "I am a strong, imaginative person, and I love the things that I create."
- "I am sure that what I offer to the world is enough."

- "I deserve to feel pleasure and have my needs fully met."
- "I feel safe expressing my sexual self in enjoyable, healthy, and creative ways."
- "I am a magnet for good, loving people who will assist me when I need them."
- "My body is perfect, and I am comfortable with who I am."
- "I am happy embracing change."
- "I will make the most of my future."
- "Each day, my joy and satisfaction with myself increases."
- "I am ready for great personal growth and deep positive change."

Solar Plexus Chakra

For the solar plexus chakra, our affirmations are concerning our self-esteem, self-control, and inner peace. This energy point is our source of willpower and inner strength, and it is our driving force. The affirmations that we will be repeating for this chakra are fantastic for boosting your confidence and hyping you up for occasions.

If you have a big presentation at work or an important college exam coming up, try using these affirmations to get yourself into the right frame of mind:

- "I'm capable, ambitious, and determined to fulfill my purpose in life."
- "I am powerful, and I am confident in my power."
- "Inner peace and confidence flow through me."
- "I believe in myself, and I feel more confident in myself every single day."
- "I don't always need to be in control, and that's okay."
- "I feel capable and driven to pursue my goals."
- "I feel no guilt for past experiences."
- "I free myself from the pain of negative past experiences."
- "I know that I am strong, good, and worthy of success."
- "I forgive myself for any previous mistakes. I will learn from them."
- "The only thing I can control is how I approach situations."

Heart Chakra

For the heart chakra, our affirmations are about loving others, feeling love ourselves, and healing past wounds. This chakra is our source of love, our ability to make important decisions, and inner peace. The affirmations that we will recite for this energy point are designed to help you overcome emotional wounds, listen to your heart when making decisions, and find inner peace in your ability to make choices for your own happiness.

- "I love who I am unconditionally, and I offer the same love to others."
- "I choose to love myself, take joy in who I am, and show compassion to myself and others."
- "I am happy and well because my heart chakra is open."
- "I am free of the wounds of my past."
- "I accept whatever form my emotions take, and I will keep control."
- "I forgive myself, and I forgive others."
- "I freely give love to others, and it makes me feel happy and whole."
- "I aim to fulfill my heart's desire every day, and I do."
- "I open myself to love, and every day I receive and give more."
- "I create healthy and loving relationships that are beneficial for all involved."

Throat Chakra

For the throat chakra, our affirmations are centered around our creativity, communication skills, and ability to turn ideas into reality. This chakra is our source of change bringing willpower, problem-solving, and people skills. Thus, all the affirmations listed below will be very useful for those of you needing a boost in social situations.

These affirmations are said to help us feel more confident in expressing ourselves and our artistry:

- "I speak the truth with ease, and others know this."
- "I trust my true voice, and I let it speak for me."
- "My thoughts and words have an impact on the world."
- "I am a caring listener and a great communicator."
- "Others listen when I speak."
- "When I speak to others, they take my opinions and contributions into account."
- "I don't second guess the words I speak. I'm confident in my thoughts."
- "Others always understand and respect me."
- "I can find the right words for any occasion."
- "My creativity has no limits and neither does my ambition."

- "I am an artist, regardless of my chosen art."

Third Eye Chakra

For the third eye chakra, our affirmations target our spiritual doubts, gut instincts, and sense of purpose in life. This chakra is the source of our spirituality and inner wisdom, and therefore, any doubts you have about your spirituality or ability to make the right decisions for yourself come from here.

The affirmations below are meant to help you feel more secure in your spirituality and intuition:

- "I follow the lead of my inner wisdom and knowledge."
- "I am following my true path in life."
- "Every day, I take a step toward fulfilling my purpose in life."
- "I listen to my intuition, and I know it will lead me down the correct path in life."
- "I know how to make the best decisions for myself, and I do it with ease."
- "I trust my third eye to guide me safely through life."
- "The world is open to me, and everything is possible."
- "It is wise and safe to follow the guidance that my third eye gives me."

- "My third eye is opening, and my full purpose will soon be revealed to me."
- "I am wise, I am intuitive, and I know what is best for me."

Crown Chakra

Lastly, for the crown chakra, our affirmations are concerning our connection to our spiritual side, our divine knowledge, and our oneness with the world around us. This chakra is most commonly associated with being the source of all the other chakras, our primary link to the spiritual world, and our source of divine knowledge and wisdom. Because of these associations, the affirmations we need to say are based around reassuring ourselves of our spirituality.

- "At this moment, I am happy, sure of myself, and aware of my worth."
- "I radiate love, I radiate joy, and I radiate light."
- "Every day, I open myself to divine guidance."
- "I am in a constant connection to my divine self."
- "We all exist in this world to make a difference."
- "I glow with love and light that attracts others who glow with love and light."

- "I feel at one with the world in which I reside."
- "I feel connected and tuned into the divine energy of the universe."
- "The world is beautiful, and I embrace this beauty in whatever form it takes."
- "I know my spiritual path, and I live my life to fulfill it."

MASSAGE

Massage is an ancient healing therapy that has been used by Indian religions since at least 3000 BCE. For thousands of years, Ayurveda practitioners have used massage to alleviate pain, heal injuries, and prevent illness. A key part of the success behind Ayurvedic massage healing comes from its effect on the chakras. Although massages are fantastic for bodily health by stimulating blood flow and relieving muscle tension, chakra massages also target the specific locations of chakras and help to relieve blockages.

By massaging specific chakras, we can reduce tension in the region, lower stress and anxiety levels, improve blood pressure, and release toxins that may be polluting the organs, muscles, and glands associated with certain chakras. Most chakra massages combine the usage of essential oils, incense, and crystal therapy for a complete chakra-healing experience.

Root Chakra

The root chakra is a very simple one to heal with massage. Because of the location of this energy point, we have the feet, legs, and glutes that can all be focused and massaged in order for this chakra to benefit. Glutes may be an awkward area to have massaged, but this region is closest to our root chakra and provides the most benefits for us. Most full body massage packages will cover the glutes. Any chakra massage package will definitely focus in this area.

Sacral Chakra

For the sacral chakra, we ideally want any massage to focus on the lower abdomen and lower back. Most commonly, sacral chakra massages pinpoint the lumbar section of the lower back, the area just below the belly button, and the hips. Oil massages around the lumbar region are particularly effective at opening up this chakra and double up as incredibly good for general back and posture health.

Solar Plexus Chakra

Massages for the solar plexus chakra usually focus on the area around the middle to upper abdomen and the middle back area. For the most part, you will see solar plexus massages happening over the area of your solar plexus in your central abdomen. Chakra massages in this area usually consist of pressured clockwise movements that are designed to activate the flow of energy in the chakra.

Heart Chakra

There are two distinct types of massage that are

effective for the heart chakra. One is traditional chakra massages, and the other is trigger point therapy. Trigger point therapy is a complex and potentially painful type of massage therapy that targets specific areas of tension. This is something that is done by a trained professional, and although it is incredibly effective for balancing this chakra, it can be painful and intense at times. Otherwise, for traditional chakra massages, you will often see these being conducted on the upper back, shoulders, and over the heart.

Throat Chakra

The throat chakra benefits mainly from massages to the back and front of the neck, jaw, and sternum. Massages involving aromatherapy are very common for this energy point. Most commonly, you will start with a deep tissue massage to the back of the neck to loosen up the area around the chakra. Following that, lighter oil massages are done from the sternum, up through the throat, and onto the jaw area. This process is the optimal way to relieve blockages and imbalances in the area of the throat chakra.

Third Eye Chakra

For the third eye chakra, there is a specific technique that is used called brow stripping. In brow stripping, long and pressured strokes are done along the length of the muscles in the brow. Often, we will also see massages for this chakra done near the ears and temples as well. Essential oils are very commonly used in this area for their beneficial effects in relieving stress and anxiety.

❁

Crown Chakra

Finally, we have the crown chakra. Typically, scalp massages are the go-to for this energy point. Scalp massages are amazing at increasing the blood flow to the brain, relieving tension in skull tissue, and relaxing muscles in the head and neck. Massages in this area typically follow the lines of the skull. By activating the blood vessels in these areas, we can greatly increase blood and energy flow to and from this chakra.

❁

COLOR THERAPY

Color therapy, also known as chromotherapy, is one of the best passive ways of healing our chakras. But, what is it, and how does it work? To put it simply, color therapy is the practice of using the frequency of colors in the world around us to promote healing in our chakras. Earlier on, in the first chapter, I had mentioned that each chakra has a color which it is visualized as. The colors associated with these chakras represent different aspects of our world. If we take one of these colors and surround ourselves with it, we allow its energy to resonate with the chakra that it represents. This flow of energy helps to heal and rebalance the chakra, and it gives us a source of energy outside of our own bodies.

There are multiple ways to carry out color therapy. The simplest and most organic way is through nature. Below I have listed some examples of using nature to heal each chakra:

- **Root Chakra**: If we want to heal our root chakra, we may want to meditate on a patch of bare soil or on a large stone. This direct connection to the reddish-brown ground below us will help the chakra absorb energy from the parts of our world that it is most deeply connected to.
- **Sacral Chakra**: For our sacral chakra, we can look to spend time around orange

areas of nature or things. Places like orange sandy beaches and citrus orchids are fantastic. Neither of those are very common depending on where you live, though. Some simpler-to-find options are fire, the orange glow of a sunset, or even a patch of autumn leaves.
- **Solar Plexus Chakra**: The solar plexus is primarily linked to the color yellow, so we want to try and surround ourselves with yellow aspects of nature. Some of these include yellow sand and yellow flowers.
- **Heart Chakra**: The heart chakra is an easy one to heal in nature with color therapy. With the primary color being green, we need to simply take a walk in a forest or meditate on some green grass.
- **Throat Chakra**: The throat chakra is another rather easy one to heal through nature. This energy point is linked to the colors blue and violet. Violet may be a bit difficult to come across in nature but blue is pretty common. In order to heal the throat chakra through interaction with nature, we can take a trip to the sea or a lake. Large bodies of water are a wealth of energy. Blue flowers are also rather common in nature and can be planted in your garden to provide a nearby source of energy.

- **Third Eye Chakra**: The third eye chakra needs purple. This may seem a bit tough to come by, but there are some pretty simple options. One of these options is lavender. This flower is very easy to come by and can be planted in any garden. Along with that, the third eye chakra has a deep connection to the moon. Moonlight is often considered to have a purple hue and meditation or walks in the glow of the moon can heal this chakra very effectively.
- **Crown Chakra**: Lastly, we will discuss the crown chakra. This energy point is represented by the colors gold and white. We may think we're out of luck unless we are rich or live in a snowy region, but don't worry—there are options open to everyone wanting to heal this chakra. The best way to heal this chakra is through the golden rays of a midday sun. Rays of light shining directly down onto our crown is the most effective way to absorb the energy of the world around us into this chakra. White flowers, snow, and chalk are examples of aspects of nature we can also use.

Aside from nature, color therapy can also very effectively be performed by wearing clothes, jewelry, and makeup in the color of the chakra we wish to empower. If we're artists, we may wish to decorate our art studio with the color blue to empower our throat chakra. In fact, decorating rooms to empower certain chakras is a very effective way of energizing our energy points during our day-to-day lives. Curtains, rugs, blankets, cushions, wall paint, and even colored lights can be used in this way to boost the energy of a room.

MUSICAL HEALING

Music has been an integral part of traditional Indian religious ceremonies for thousands of years. Music, as with color, gives off powerful spiritual energy. Just as with every chakra, there is a corresponding color, each chakra has a corresponding type of sound too.

- **Root Chakra**: For the Muladhara chakra, the sound of large drums are most closely linked. These bass-filled sounds imitate the noise made by earth and rock moving.
- **Sacral Chakra**: The sacral chakra is represented by the sounds of small drums. Small drums mimic the sounds of movement and activity, the stomping of feet, and the rhythm of love-making.
- **Solar Plexus Chakra**: Trumpets and large wind instruments affect the solar plexus chakra. These instruments imitate the sounds of our stomach, and it is believed that the breath used to play them originates in that area.
- **Heart Chakra**: Strings have their influence on the heart chakra. There is a reason "pulling on my heart strings" is a commonly used phrase. Anyone who has heard a brilliant violinist play can confirm the effect those instruments have on their heart.
- **Throat Chakra**: Small wind instruments

such as flutes and pipes are representative of the throat. These instruments mimic the action of talking and require great control over one's breathing to fully utilize.
- **Third Eye Chakra**: The third eye chakra is a fan of bells and the sounds of nature, like bird song and dripping water. These calming sounds help us focus which, in turn, empowers this chakra.
- **Crown Chakra**: The crown chakra values all of the instruments put together as one. Just as we need all the other energy points to be balanced for our crown chakra to feel balanced, we need all instruments played as one for our crown chakra to gain from them.

If we watch any Indian rituals, we will see this in action. In temples, during ceremony, the large drums are furthest to the back and sides. Then come the smaller drums, and just in front of them are the large wind instruments. Next come the strings and small wind instruments. And lastly, in the very center, are the bells, which are often held by the ceremony leader.

For those of us who don't have access to temples and ceremonies, there are plenty of resources available online and in CD form. Many people like to use classical music during meditation to empower certain chakras. One of Mozart's piano concertos, for example, may be exactly what you need to open up your heart chakra. Similarly, a full orchestral piece may help to center your crown chakra. There is plenty of modern music also made for the specific goal of empowering and healing the chakras. Feel free to explore and experiment. Musical healing works wonders for me, and it may work wonders for you too.

REIKI

Reiki is an ancient Japanese healing technique that has been practiced throughout East Asia for centuries under various names. The core belief around reiki is that we have the ability to manipulate, move, and transfer vital life energy (ki, chi, prana) in ourselves and others to heal physical and spiritual aspects of our bodies.

A trained reiki master can help us heal and balance our chakras by radiating their energy into our chakra centers through the palms of their hands. In a physical sense, reiki is different from massage in that the touches are very light and non-invasive. The primary goal of reiki isn't to encourage physical changes like blood flow or muscle relaxation, but rather to directly energize the chakras.

A skilled reiki practitioner can energize chakras that are starved of energy, divert the energy from overactive chakras into other parts of the body, and free up blockages that are stopping the movement of energy up the spine.

CHAPTER 4
FOODS AND CHAKRAS

Food is one of our most primal needs as human beings. This deep, intrinsic link that we have to food has both physical and spiritual aspects, especially in regards to our chakras. The colors of many foods help to describe their mineral and vitamin contents. For example, red foods are very high in certain antioxidants which cause the red coloration. These antioxidants also happen to be very good for gut and bowel health, and as such they directly influence the area around our root chakra.

Similarly, the specific type of antioxidants found in berries and other deep blue or purple foods are particularly good for improving memory, cognitive function, and defending the brain against deterioration. These foods are the ones most closely linked with our third eye chakra for these exact reasons.

THE RELATIONSHIP BETWEEN CHAKRAS AND FOOD

Root Chakra

Of all the chakras, the root chakra is the one most easily healed and balanced through food. All foods naturally come from the earth, and so all have at least some energy from the earth in them. This earth energy is what powers the root chakra and helps it to maintain balance. Because of how easy this chakra is to nourish, if you simply make sure to eat healthy, well-balanced meals on a regular basis, this is often enough to keep it open and relatively unblocked.

However, if we do need to focus on specific root chakra foods to help heal the chakra or unblock it, we should look toward red foods and root vegetables. Because earth is an element responsible for building structure, these foods may cause a large increase in body mass if eaten in too high of quantities. As in all things in life, moderation is key.

Take a look below at some examples of foods that can help keep your root chakra balanced:

- Meat
- Red peppers
- Tomato
- Pomegranate
- Chillies
- Red berries
- Beetroot
- Garlic

- Red apple

Sacral Chakra

As we have already covered, the sacral chakra is our source of sensual energy and passion. This specific chakra is responsible for our energy in romance and in passion projects. So whether you are making love, playing your favorite sport, or playing your chosen instrument, the foods associated with this energy point will give you the boost you need. This boost comes from the high electrolyte and vitamin content of these foods, when we sweat or spend long periods of time in deep focus, we quickly burn through our body's supply of vitamins and minerals.

All the foods associated with this chakra are dense in the vitamins and minerals needed to replenish our reserves; in many cases, they contain plenty of refreshing liquid for your body, too. Here are some of these foods:

- Carrot
- Peach
- Apricot
- Orange
- Mango
- Pumpkin
- Mandarin
- Peanuts

- Tofu

***

Solar Plexus Chakra

The solar plexus chakra is our body's primary source of vital energy. The foods associated with this energy point are, as such, packed full of the energy that is needed to power us as we go about our daily routine. Foods high in carbohydrates, the human body's primary energy source, like grains, potatoes, and meaty fruits are excellent sources of raw energy for our body. This raw energy is then distributed where it is needed by the solar plexus.

As well as carb-heavy foods, the solar plexus chakra is also linked to pungent and strong-flavored foods. These foods are believed to contain the fire of vital energy. Some of these vital energy-flavored foods include ginger, lemon, and peppers. Other foods that are ideal for strengthening the solar plexus chakra are as follows:

- Grains
- Ginger
- Pineapple
- Banana
- Yellow pear
- Lemon
- Yellow peppers
- Potato

Heart Chakra

The heart chakra is a big fan of green foods. Green foods, in general, tend to be very high in fiber, as well as essential minerals. These are absolutely crucial to the health of our heart and vascular system. Fiber helps us to regulate our blood sugar levels, which play a huge part in our heart health and in balancing the flow of energy in and out of the heart chakra.

The minerals from these plants, on the other hand, are crucial for maintaining the health of our organs and blood vessels. Perhaps you are wondering why this is. Well, without the right cocktail of minerals, our blood vessels would be unable to transport oxygen, glucose, and vital energy around our body to the other organs and chakras.

Here are some of the foods that are wonderful for supporting the heart chakra:

- Watermelon
- Cucumber
- Zucchini
- Kiwi
- Avocado
- Green apple
- Mint
- Green grapes
- Leafy green vegetables

Throat Chakra

At this point, the chakras become less based on the physical body and more ethereal. This means that foods have less of a direct impact on the body and more of an impact on the soul. In a way, their effect is less tangible and more symbolic.

For our throat chakra, we want to mainly consume liquids. This energy point is heavily associated with water and the fluidity of communication and expression. Because of that, liquids and sea plants make fantastic foods to satisfy the spiritual needs of this chakra. Figs are also linked to this chakra because of their association with the Hindu god Vishnu, who was born under a fig tree. Vishnu is a creator, and the throat chakra represents our creativity.

Here are some of the foods and liquids you can incorporate into your diet if you wish to maintain a healthy throat chakra:

- Fruit juices
- Figs
- Seaweed
- Herbal tea
- Coconut water
- Soups
- Fish

Third Eye Chakra

The third eye chakra is located in the forehead—more specifically around the frontal lobe. This is the area of our brain that is responsible for emotions, problem-solving, language, memory, and judgment. All of the foods associated with this energy point are incredibly beneficial to this area of the brain, as they all contain a potent cocktail of useful antioxidants that protect against mental decay.

Blackberries and elderberries specifically are famed for their amazing benefits when it comes to mental cognizance and improving memory. Purple is one of the most powerful colors for color therapy. This is because the richness and depth of it helps to nourish the third eye chakra very efficiently. Thus, surrounding ourselves with foods of this color has a second effect of being a form of color therapy.

Take a look below at some ideas for foods you can eat to benefit your third eye chakra:

- Sweet potatoes
- Plums
- Red grapes
- Aubergine
- Prunes
- Passionfruit
- Blackberries
- Purple cabbage
- Elderberries

Crown Chakra

Finally, our crown chakra is a completely ethereal and spiritual chakra. Thus, no foods affect it as it is free from any earthly bonds. Fasting is viewed as the easiest and most effective way of purifying and unblocking this energy point. Fasting has long been viewed as a holy practice among many ancient religions, and now science is starting to recognize the benefits of it as well.

Intermittent fasting has become a regular fixture in many modern eating regimes. By taking short fasting periods of 24-36 hours, one allows the body to naturally detoxify itself, flush out toxins, and burn its natural reserves of energy. By fasting, you can also clear the mind by making your body slow down its energy production. Too much energy can cause an overactive mind and make it very hard for an individual to focus.

Sunlight, fresh air, and the ambience of nature also help to nourish this spiritual chakra. These are all outside sources of energy which our crown chakra can tap into:

- Purified water
- Sunlight
- Fresh air
- Nature
- Fasting
- Detoxing

DETOXING AND FASTING

Fasting has been a core concept of spiritualism in many cultures over thousands of years. Everyone from Tibetan Buddhists to Native American shamans and new age Pagans have noticed the incredible benefits of fasting and its effects on detoxing the body. Not only have spiritualists seen improvements, doctors, scientists, and dietitians across the world have taken notice of the potential benefits of frequent short-term fasting.

By practicing intermittent fasting, you can open yourself up to all of these amazing benefits:

- **Stabilize blood sugar levels**: By fasting regularly, you allow your body to naturally regulate its blood sugar levels by giving it periods to drain any excess blood sugar.
- **Lower insulin resistance**: During periods of fasting, the body drains itself of blood sugar. This means the cells that would usually use insulin to process that blood sugar are given a break. When you introduce sugar and insulin to these cells again later on, their resistance is lower and, in turn, they work more efficiently.
- **Reduce inflammation**: Chronic inflammation is a serious issue that many people face due to unhealthy diets. This form of persistent inflammation is one of

the leading causes of heart disease, cancer, and various forms of arthritis. By fasting, you allow your body time to drain itself of the toxins which can cause chronic inflammation to flare up.
- **Balancing of blood pressure and cholesterol levels**: Cholesterol is one of the leading causes of high blood pressure among adults. By fasting, you allow your body time to remove blockages and toxins from your blood which may otherwise cause high blood pressure. Consistent high blood pressure leads to serious cardiovascular diseases.
- **Larger amounts of growth hormone production**: Human growth hormone, which is also known as HGH, is the key hormone responsible for growth, metabolism, muscle strength, and weight loss. A number of studies have shown that fasting naturally increases the amount of HGH that is produced by the body.
- **Helps with weight loss and increased metabolism**: By fasting, you can obviously lower your overall calorie intake. This will lead to weight loss over the long-term. In the short-term, on the other hand, fasting can help boost your metabolism by increasing production of the neurotransmitter norepinephrine.

- **Increases brain function and mental clarity**: Fasting has been shown to encourage the production of nerve cells in the brain. Scientists are not exactly sure why this happens, but they know it directly improves the function of your brain and enhances mental clarity over a long period of time.

All of these benefits have been proven by science, and true to the theme of the crown chakra, they all affect our other six energy points in amazing ways.

Similar to fasting, detoxing is another way of helping the chakras heal and rebalance. Detoxing is simply the process of cutting any potentially toxin-causing foods out of your diet for a certain period of time. The longer you keep them out of your diet, the better the effectiveness of the detox.

Food-based toxins can be one of the leading causes in chakra blockages, and they are getting even more common in today's world of fast food and constant snacking. In order to detox effectively, there are some simple steps to follow and adhere to. Take a look at them below:

- Reduce or eliminate your alcohol consumption.
- Get eight hours of uninterrupted sleep every night.
- Drink more water; around half a gallon a day is recommended.

- Try to reduce or eliminate sugar and processed foods from your diet.
- Consume a lot of antioxidant-rich foods.
- Consume more fiber-rich foods.
- Reduce your amount of salt consumption.
- Exercise for at least 30 minutes every day.

CHAPTER 5
ESSENTIAL OILS AND CHAKRAS

I'm sure many of you who are reading this are familiar with essential oils and their overall health benefits. However, for those of you who are not so familiar or would like to learn more, let me give you a quick run-down.

Essential oils are extracts of various flowers, trees, roots, and herbs that have some absolutely amazing health benefits. Inside of these plants are particular compounds that have unique aromatic essences. These essences are distilled into an oil via distillation or cold pressing. This oil is then infused with a carrier oil in order to dilute it to manageable amounts. After this, it is ready for use. Essential oils are completely natural; anything that is made through chemical processes is *not* an authentic essential oil, so stay clear of these.

AROMATHERAPY

Aromatherapy is the most common way through which people make use of essential oils. The concept of aromatherapy is simple: we use aromatic essential oils to medicinally improve the health of the mind, body, and spirit.

For thousands of years, humans have made use of this practice. In fact, it is one of the oldest and most widespread medical techniques in existence. Ancient peoples in China, Egypt, and India all extensively made use of incense, balms, and oils that contain the essential oils of various medicinal plants. The precursor to modern essential oil distillation is attributed to the 10th century Persians, although it is almost certain that similar practices had been around before then.

Since at least the 12th century, it was common practice in many German abbeys to distill essential oils from sage, lavender, and rosemary for medicinal purposes. In the early half of the 15th century, the Swiss physician and father of toxicology, Paracelsus, extensively documented the utilization of essential oils in his experiments based around alchemy. In the 16th century, the first mentions of essential oils started popping up in German literature. Even up to the modern day, essential oils are a recognized form of therapy for multiple ailments and discomforts, and combining them with our knowledge of chakras can be incredibly life changing.

So, how does aromatherapy work? Well, there are

two primary ways in which aromatherapy works: through smell and through skin absorption. There are a variety of products that help us with this and add to the usefulness of the oils that we are using. Some of the product types we will often run into are diffusers, bathing salts, hot and cold compresses, clay masks, and body creams, lotions, and oils. Be careful to only buy oils from reputable sources since they are not regulated by the FDA.

ESSENTIAL OILS FOR CHAKRA HEALING

Root Chakra

- Patchouli
- Ginger
- Frankincense
- Vetiver root
- Atlas cedarwood
- Australian sandalwood

Sacral Chakra

- Ylang ylang
- Geranium
- Bergamot
- Rose absolute
- Clary sage
- Sweet orange

Solar Plexus Chakra

- Juniper berry
- Cypress
- Rosemary
- Lime
- Lemon
- Fennel

Heart Chakra

- Fragonia
- Rose otto
- Tea tree
- May chang
- Melissa
- Jasmine

Throat Chakra

- Melaleuca
- Chamomile
- Basil
- Peppermint
- Spearmint
- Blue cypress

Third Eye Chakra

- Sage
- Rosemary
- Helichrysum
- Marjoram
- Sandalwood
- Eucalyptus

Crown Chakra

- Myrrh
- Lavender
- Patchouli
- Bergamot

- Fragonia
- Frankincense

WHERE TO USE OUR CHAKRA OILS

Now that we know what essential oils are suited to each chakra, we need to figure out where to actually utilize them. Each chakra has multiple points where we can place our essential oils depending on the ailments that our imbalances cause or the areas we want to give a boost to.

- **Root Chakra:** As we have already covered, the root chakra is tightly linked to our feet, legs, and bowels. The ginger essential oil is a powerful anti-inflammatory and can be used to help reduce joint pain in the feet and legs. Patchouli and vetiver have calming effects and can be used on the bowl region to calm an overactive root chakra. Cedarwood, sandalwood, and frankincense are all balancing essential oils that we can use at the base of the feet, behind the knees, and at the base of the spine to maintain normal function and level balance.
- **Sacral Chakra:** Being very closely connected to our sexual organs and emotional links to people, this chakra can

easily fall into imbalance without regular attendance. We can help open up a blocked sacral chakra by placing some bergamot or rose absolute just below our navel. An overactive sacral chakra can be slowed by placing some ylang-ylang or clary sage on the lower back or hips. And lastly, we can help to maintain balance of this chakra by using some sweet orange or geranium in a vertical line below the navel.

- **Solar Plexus Chakra:** As we mentioned earlier, the solar plexus chakra is located just above the navel in the center of the torso. For a blocked solar plexus chakra, we will need to place juniper berry or fennel in a vertical line just above the navel. If we have an overactive chakra, we can place some cypress or rosemary in the middle of the spine or above the navel. Lastly, we can maintain a balanced chakra by placing some lime or lemon above our navel in a circle or over our ribs.
- **Heart Chakra:** Being our emotional center, this chakra can be turbulent and quick to fall into imbalance. To help unblock this energy point, we want to use rose otto or fragonia over the central chest area. These are powerful anti-inflammatories that can help combat back and chest pain, and they also work toward rebalancing the heart chakra. Tea tree and melissa are both

fantastic for calming an overactive heart chakra and should be placed between the shoulder blades. Finally, jasmine and may chang can be used very effectively to maintain balance of the chakra and help ward off negative emotions.

- **Throat Chakra:** As our communications center, this energy point is primarily based in our throat, lungs, and mouth area. Melaleuca, basil, and blue cypress oil are particularly good for cleansing the skin around the face and chest of acne and other skin conditions that may be brought on by an unbalanced throat chakra. Chamomile oil is used to calm an overactive throat chakra by placing some just below the chin. Lastly, peppermint and spearmint oil are fantastic for clearing blocked sinuses and soothing sore throats. Simply rub some around your nose or under your chin.
- **Third Eye Chakra:** For the third eye chakra, we are primarily looking to help with headaches, boosting our mood, and decreasing stress. For reducing the frequency and pain from headaches, we can use helichrysum, marjoram, and eucalyptus oil. We can apply these oils over the sinuses, behind the ears, and at the base of the neck. For boosting mood and reducing stress, we want to apply sage, rosemary, or sandalwood to our

forehead or below the chin, or we can inhale it in vapor form.
- **Crown Chakra:** Finally, the crown chakra has very few links to the physical body. Thus, nearly all of the benefits we will get from using oils for this energy point are mental in nature. For insomnia and anxiety, myrrh, lavender, and patchouli oil are fantastic at helping us relax and sleep soundly when inhaled or placed on the forehead. To help boost moods and aid the flow of spiritual energy, frankincense, bergamot, and fragonia oil are all incredibly effective when inhaled or placed on the temples.

CHAPTER 6
CRYSTALS AND CHAKRAS

CRYSTALS FOR CHAKRA HEALING

Crystal healing is one of the most popular and straightforward forms of healing chakras. Along with being quite simple, crystal healing has been shown to be incredibly effective in rebalancing and encouraging healing in the chakras. Although there is little scientific research regarding the effects of crystals, it is clear that something is at work behind the scenes.

The traditional belief is that crystals work as conduits for energy. They are superconductors that allow positive and negative energy to flow through them incredibly effectively. Combine that conductivity with the correct colors for each chakra, and you essentially have a battery pack for every one of the energy points.

As well as being incredible sources of energy for our chakras, crystals can act as amazing cleansing tools. They behave like sponges for bad energy. If we feel that a chakra is blocked, we can place one of the corresponding gemstones on it and attempt to drain any negative energy from it, then replacing it with positive energy from the crystal.

A common theme is to describe the energy coming from crystals as vibrations. When something bad happens to us, it is an imbalance of too many low frequency vibrations. Low frequency vibrations cause our chakras to slow their spin or even become blocked. High frequency vibrations, on the other hand, speed up our chakras and re-energize them. These specific frequencies are found in all crystals.

Keep in mind that different crystals do have varying effects and work effectively in different areas of the body. The color of the various crystals corresponds to the colors of our chakras, and as such, those crystals help those specific areas of the body and the mental aspects of those particular chakras.

There are two basic techniques for healing the different regions of our body: targeted healing and general healing.

- **Targeted Healing**: For targeted healing, we try to pinpoint the specific location of the issue. If your stresses are manifesting as knee pain, you would place crystals alongside the knee on either side. Similarly, if negative energy manifests as bowel issues, you would place crystals on your lower stomach.

- **General Healing**: For general healing, we take a direct approach to covering the chakra center itself. In this technique, we focus on balancing the chakra first and foremost, and hopefully by balancing the source, any other issues will also clear up.

Most of the time, I would recommend doing a combination of both techniques when trying to treat specific issues or chakras. If you are only doing some routine maintenance, however, general healing is usually the best option.

※

Root Chakra
When working with root chakra crystals, we are mainly aiming to improve the health of the lower body and our sense of security. The root chakra has the potential to be a hiding place for a lot of negative energy. Any feelings of lack of security regarding basic needs goes here. If you're worried about rent or grocery money, or if you are experiencing fear regarding your general health, all of that stress will soak into this chakra and manifest into issues surrounding this area.

Targeted healing areas for this chakra are typically found on the tops of the feet, the ankles, either side of the knees, the inside of the thighs, and the lower abdomen over the bowl.

Here are some of the best crystals to utilize if you want to balance your root chakra:

- Bloodstone
- Zircon
- Hematite
- Fire agate
- Black tourmaline
- Garnet

Sacral Chakra

Sacral chakra crystals are an incredibly potent form of crystal due to their brilliant colors and pure sensual energy. This chakra can be a source of a lot of personal negative energy. Due to the very personal nature of this energy point, any personal insecurities, embarrassing feelings, and sexual shames may end up poisoning the sacral chakra. Any kind of personal insecurities about body size, appearance, or sexuality can manifest in blockages of this energy point, and these blockages can lead to further issues in the areas surrounding this chakra.

Targeted healing areas for this chakra are the sides of the hips, on the lumbar of the spine, and above the sexual organs on the pubis.

The best crystals for the sacral chakra are as follows:

- Carnelian

- Copper
- Turquoise
- Orange fluorite
- Imperial topaz
- Moonstone

Solar Plexus Chakra

Solar plexus crystals are a particularly strong source of life energy. Some ancient cultures believed these yellow crystals to be sunrays in physical form. Maybe they had a point, because these crystals are incredibly effective at kickstarting our solar plexus chakra, the source of life energy in the body. Due to the nature of this chakra, any feelings of depression, lethargy, amotivation, and lack of willpower will linger in the energy point and affect its ability to produce energy for us.

The careful placement of some of these stones can massively help to rid the chakra of those damaging energies. Some of the targeted healing points for this chakra are along the sides of the ribs, on the solar plexus, on the center of the spine, and on the inside of the elbows.

Here are the ideal crystals to use for this chakra:

- Amber
- Yellow jasper
- Tiger's eye
- Yellow apatite

- Citrine
- Honey calcite

Heart Chakra

Heart chakra crystals are some of the most popular crystals out there for their effects not only in helping our love lives but also our cardiovascular health. This is the only chakra that has two different color crystals which represent its physical and mental aspects. Pink crystals represent its mental aspects while green crystals represent physical aspects of this energy point. Pink is a warm, nurturing color. It is the color of newborns, newly budded roses, and sweet berries. This color and its crystals help to combat negative energies surrounding love and relationships.

Past trauma from relationships, commitment issues, and fears of abandonment all manifest in this chakra and can be removed with pink crystals. Green, on the other hand, is the color of health in nature; green plants are healthy plants. It is the color of life and prosperity. Negative energy in this chakra can manifest as cardiovascular issues.

The accurate placement of crystals on this chakra and its targeted healing spots can help imbue some of that healthy life energy into it. The targeted healing areas for this chakra are the sternum (over the heart if using pink gems), between the shoulders and collar bones, in the crook of the armpit, and on the upper spine.

The following crystals can greatly benefit this chakra:

- Rose quartz
- Green aventurine
- Malachite
- Jade
- Pink tourmaline
- Rosasite

Throat Chakra

Crystals associated with this energy point have powerful creative energies to them. Lapis lazuli, in particular, has been used for thousands of years as a paint and dye by artists and crafters across the globe. Negative energies in this chakra focus on suppressing our creative elements and our ability to express ourselves. Because of this chakra being our source of creativity, any feelings of creative insecurity, stage-fright, or artist's block can stem from imbalances here.

In regards to physical ailments, negative energy here can manifest as throat infections, neck pain, and thyroid dysfunctions, among other things. Our targeted healing points for this chakra are on either side of the neck, in our jugular notch, below the chin, and at the back of the neck.

The best crystals for balancing the throat chakra include the following:

- Angelite
- Amazonite
- Aquamarine
- Celestite
- Lapis lazuli
- Blue calcite

Third Eye Chakra

The crystals associated with this chakra are filled with frequencies that resonate very efficiently with those of our brain waves. Because of this resonance, these crystals can have an amazing brain-boosting effect for us.

The negative energies that affect our third eye chakra can not only cause anxiety, depression, and confusion, but they may also bring on migraines, mental fog, and even dizziness. The utilization of crystals to cleanse this chakra can help treat all these issues and also improve the health of our brain to an even higher level than before.

Targeted healing areas of this chakra are between the eyebrows, on the temples, behind the ears, and at the top of the brain stem.

Some of the crystals associated with the third eye chakra are listed below:

- Azurite
- Tanzanite
- Amethyst
- Obsidian
- Purple fluorite
- Lolite

Crown Chakra

Finally, we will discuss the crown chakra and its crystals. The crystals associated with this chakra are especially pure, containing energy that is untainted by any negative frequencies. They act as especially powerful conduits and can actually substitute for the crystals of other chakras too. This is due to the crown chakra's role as the source of all energy points. This chakra is the home of our spiritual energy and is the primary entry point of divine light and knowledge.

Because of the spiritual importance of this chakra, it's somewhere which can easily be affected by negative energies, meaning it is crucial that we cleanse this area frequently. Regular crystal cleanses in this region can help to prevent the spiritual doubt, tainted wisdom, and misdirection that is brought on by blockages here.

The most effective way of performing targeted healing for this chakra is by laying down and creating a halo of crystals around your head. This energy point is not a physical chakra, so it doesn't help to have its crystals in contact with the body.

Here are the crystals you can utilize to help balance your crown chakra:

- Quartz crystal
- White topaz
- Selenite
- White danburite
- Diamond
- White howlite

SETTING UP FOR CRYSTAL HEALING

Regardless of whether you are performing the healing on yourself or on someone else, it is incredibly important that everyone involved gets into a state of deep relaxation. We can achieve this by playing calming, melodious ambient music, diffusing essential oils into the air, burning incense, making sure the room is warm, and dimming the lights to a comfortably low level.

Once we have an ideal environment, everyone involved should take some meditative breaths in order to fall into a state of deeper relaxation. Continue to breathe in this manner throughout the process. If you are placing crystals on yourself, it's especially important that you make sure you're calm. Chakras are their most open and malleable when you're calm and relaxed, so it's key that you make sure you are in this state in order to get the best results out of your crystal healing.

How Long to Use

Crystal healing sessions can last as long as you feel you can maintain focus. If you can continue your calm breathing and stay focused on healing your chakras, you will be making an impact. Whether you only have five minutes or a whole hour to work with, you will be making a positive impact on your health.

Keep in mind that you should not force anything. If you feel yourself getting anxious or like you *have* to continue going, then stop. Forcing the process will only create stress and anxiety which will worsen any imbalance you already feel.

Allow yourself as much time as you need, and relish the deep relaxation. The length of the session is less important than the depth of relaxation that is achieved during the session.

Cleansing Crystals

Before and after each session, we must be sure to cleanse our crystals. As I mentioned earlier, crystals tend to soak up both negative and positive energies. We can cleanse the negative energies and purify our stones after and before each session to maximize their effectiveness.

Cleansing crystals is a simple process. We can easily do it by passing them under cold, running water, smudging them with sage smoke, or enveloping them in incense smoke.

USING CRYSTALS IN OUR DAILY LIVES

Along with being beautiful and useful in cleansing sessions, crystals are also functional in more practical ways. We can actually incorporate them into many of our daily routines and keep a little source of positive energy with us at all times.

- **Using crystals during meditation**: We've already covered the wonders of chakra meditation, but we can enhance both the effects of meditation and of our crystals by using them in tandem. Placing crystals around you or on chakra points during meditation can allow you to absorb even more energy and cleanse more efficiently.
- **Carry crystals with us**: Carrying crystals with you, whether it be in your pockets or as a piece of jewelry, can be a very handy and effective way of staying connected to a source of positive energy at all times. If you're looking to work on a specific chakra, wearing a necklace of one of that chakra's crystals will allow you to soak up that energy all day long. If you're particularly prone to anxiety during your day, wearing a crystal and helps you feel relaxed can help combat that.
- **Creating a crystal grid**: Crystal grids are a creative and aesthetically pleasing way of arranging your crystals in your house or

garden. There are many sacred geometric patterns that mimic the shape of various chakras and sacred features of ancient medicine. By arranging our crystals into these grids, we can amplify their effects and introduce a hub of positive energy into our environment.
- **Create a crystal altar**: Similar to the crystal grid, we can create an altar inside of our living space. This altar will consist of incense, crystals, sacred idols, and even offerings to our chakras. We can meditate and perform crystal healing at this altar to increase our spiritual energy and our sensitivity to divine energy.
- **Use crystals in your home decor**: Using crystals in your home decor is one of the best ways of passively improving the vibe of your living space. Try incorporating the crystals that you need into wallhangings, lampshades, ornaments, plant pots, and even cutlery.
- **Use them while you sleep**: We can incorporate crystals into our bedroom too. Try placing a crystal on your headboard or under your pillow. You can also place crystals under the mattress, especially in areas where you want to cleanse specific chakras.
- **Use crystals in your self-care routine**: Lastly, using crystals in your self-care

routine can be a fantastic, intimate way of treating yourself with positive energy and self-love. Try adding crystals into your bath and the water you use to wash your face. You can even place crystals in with your creams and skincare products to infuse them with positive energy.

CHAPTER 7
THINGS YOU NEED TO KNOW

FAQ

We've been through so much in this book so far, and now that we're nearing the end, I'd hate to leave you with more questions than answers. So, let's try to address any outstanding questions in this FAQ. I hope that I can quell any remaining doubts you may have and finally set you on the path to enlightenment with all the knowledge you may ever need.

- **Do men and women have the same chakras?** Yes. All human beings have the same chakras regardless of sexuality, race, or origin. Although, our chakras themselves do have masculine and feminine qualities. The root, solar plexus, and throat chakras are masculine. The sacral, heart, and third eye chakras are

feminine. The crown chakra does not have a gendered quality.
- **I've heard about lower and upper chakras, but what are they?** As we know, there are seven chakras. The central chakra is the heart. The three above that are sometimes called the upper chakras, and the three below that are sometimes known as the lower chakras.
- **Is it possible to feel my chakras?** Not in the sense that you could touch one, but often we do feel our chakras at work. Have you ever felt those butterflies in your stomach when you're with your partner? That's your sacral chakra. How about that nagging feeling in your head that you should do something? That's your third eye chakra.
- **Where can I get crystals?** You can find crystals on many online stores that ship across the USA and the world. You almost certainly have one in your state. Try to make sure your crystals are sourced from environmentally responsible suppliers if possible.
- **Where can I get essential oils?** Similarly to crystals, there are plenty of online stores that sell real essential oils. Make sure to check that the store you buy from sources their oils responsibly and have ethical business practices. Unfortunately, the

essential oil market has a handful of MLMs (Pyramid Schemes) which operate with predatory practices, so make sure to do your research.

- **Am I crazy for believing this?** Definitely not! Society may have you believe that this is quackery and that none of it works. However, for thousands of years, millions of people have practiced these techniques and beliefs. Don't let an ignorant society stop you from reaching enlightenment.

CHAPTER 8
OTHER BOOKS BY THE AUTHOR

Here's a list of Emily Oddo books you can find on Amazon:
   Yoga for Beginners
   Chakras for Beginners
   Reiki For Beginners
   Third Eye Awakening

AFTERWORD

Finally, we reach the end of this book. We've gone from spiritual saplings desperately trying to grow up toward the sunlight to fully grown trees freely experiencing all the rays of the sun and the freedom that comes from being above the canopy of the forest. It has been quite a long journey, and we have covered a lot of information along the way. I only hope that I have given you the tools you need to take the remaining steps for yourself. Your chakras are in your own hands, as they always have been; the only difference now is that you have the knowledge to take care of them and reap their rewards.

Just remember: stay calm, focus on your goals, and never give up. With the knowledge you have learned here, you can change your life in so many ways. You have learned to love yourself and others more than ever before. You have learned to express yourself in ways you never even dreamed of. You have learned to cope with trauma in the healthiest way possible. With the knowledge of chakra healing, you have become self-sufficient in self-care. So, now you can take your knowledge out into the world and truly prosper.

REFERENCES

American Heart Association. (2019, November 25). *Regular fasting could lead to longer, healthier life*. Www.Heart.org. https://www.heart.org/en/news/2019/11/25/regular-fasting-could-lead-to-longer-healthier-life

Chakras.net. (n.d.). *Shiva and Shakti*. Www.Chakras.net. Retrieved December 12, 2020, from https://www.chakras.net/yoga-principles/shiva-and-shakti

Cronkleton, E. (2018, May 15). *Aromatherapy Uses and Benefits*. Healthline; Healthline Media. https://www.healthline.com/health/what-is-aromatherapy

Empress Organics. (2017, May 5). *Balancing Your Chakras With Essential Oils*. Empress Organics. https://empressorganics.net/blogs/news/balancing-your-chakras-with-essential-oils

Fondin, M. (2015a, February 10). *Open Yourself to Love With the Fourth Chakra*. The Chopra Center.

https://chopra.com/articles/open-yourself-to-love-with-the-fourth-chakra

Fondin, M. (2015b, April 23). *Speak Your Inner Truth With the Fifth Chakra*. Chopra. https://www.chopra.com/articles/speak-your-inner-truth-with-the-fifth-chakra

Fondin, M. (2015c, May 26). *Trust Your Intuition With the Sixth Chakra*. Chopra. https://www.chopra.com/articles/trust-your-intuition-with-the-sixth-chakra

Fondin, M. (2015d, June 4). *Connect to the Divine With the Seventh Chakra*. Chopra. https://www.chopra.com/articles/connect-to-the-divine-with-the-seventh-chakra

Fondin, M. (2020, October 7). *The Root Chakra: Muladhara*. Chopra. https://chopra.com/articles/the-root-chakra-muladhara

Frawley, D. (n.d.). *Opening the Chakras: New Myths & Old Truths*. Yogainternational.com. Retrieved December 12, 2020, from https://yogainternational.com/article/view/opening-the-chakras-new-myths-old-truths

Frawley, D. (2009). Inner Tantric Yoga: Working with the Universal Shakti: Secrets of Mantras, Deities and Meditation. In *Google Books*. Lotus Press. https://books.google.co.za/books?id=T6Vp_rTWkAAC&pg=PA163&redir_esc=y#v=onepage&q&f=false

Hurst, K. (2017a, October 19). *Heart Chakra Healing For Beginners: How To Open Your Heart Chakra*. The Law Of Attraction. https://www.thelawofattraction.com/heart-Chakra-healing/

Hurst, K. (2017b, October 19). *Root Chakra Healing For Beginners: How To Open Your Root Chakra*. The Law Of Attraction. https://www.thelawofattraction.com/root-chakra-healing/

Hurst, K. (2017c, October 19). *Sacral Chakra Healing For Beginners: How To Open Your Sacral Chakra*. The Law Of Attraction. https://www.thelawofattraction.com/sacral-chakra-healing/

Hurst, K. (2017d, October 19). *Solar Plexus Chakra Healing: How To Open Your Solar Plexus Chakra*. The Law Of Attraction. https://www.thelawofattraction.com/solar-plexus-chakra-healing/

Hurst, K. (2017e, October 19). *Third Eye Chakra Healing For Beginners: How To Open Your Third Eye*. The Law Of Attraction. https://www.thelawofattraction.com/third-eye-chakra-healing/

Hurst, K. (2017f, October 19). *Throat Chakra Healing For Beginners: How To Open Your Throat Chakra*. The Law Of Attraction. https://www.thelawofattraction.com/throat-chakra-healing/

King, D. (2018, March 27). *Chakra Foods for Healing & Health - Blog*. Deborah King. https://deborahking.com/7-foods-to-heal-7-chakras/

Lindberg, S. (2020, August 24). *What Are Chakras? Meaning, Location, and How to Unblock Them*. Healthline. https://www.healthline.com/health/what-are-chakras

Lizzy. (2013a). *How To Select The Right Chakra Stone*. Chakras.Info. https://www.chakras.info/chakra-stones/

Lizzy. (2013b). *Know Your Sacral Chakra And How*

To Harness Its Power. Chakras.Info. https://www.chakras.info/sacral-chakra/

Lizzy. (2013c). *Know Your Throat Chakra And How To Unlock Its Power*. Chakras.Info. https://www.chakras.info/throat-chakra/

Lizzy. (2019a). *7 Chakra Crash Course: A Beginner's Guide To Awakening Your Seven Chakras*. Chakras.Info. https://www.chakras.info/7-chakras/

Lizzy. (2019b, December 9). *3 Simple Yoga Poses To Activate Your Crown Chakra*. Chakras.Info. https://www.chakras.info/crown-chakra-yoga-poses/

Lizzy. (2020, April 9). *Know Your Crown Chakra And How To Tap Into Its Power*. Chakras.Info. https://www.chakras.info/crown-chakra/

McNally, R. (n.d.). *Reiki & The Chakras - Bring the Body into Balance & Harmony*. The Thirsty Soul. Retrieved December 12, 2020, from https://thethirstysoul.com/reiki/chakras-reiki/

Rosen, R. (2017, May 15). *Reclining Bound Angle Pose*. Yoga Journal. https://www.yogajournal.com/poses/reclining-bound-angle-pose

Shah, P. (2020, August 20). *A Primer of the Chakra System*. Chopra. https://www.chopra.com/articles/what-is-a-chakra

Singh Khalsa, K. P. (2016, September 9). *Chakra Massage*. MassageTherapy.com. https://www.massagetherapy.com/articles/chakra-massage

Spear, H. E. (2019, September 9). *What Is Color Therapy & How Can It Help Heal Our Chakras?* Mindbodygreen. https://www.mindbodygreen.com/articles/what-is-color-therapy-and-how-can-it-help-heal-our-chakras

Thorpe, M. (2020, October 27). *12 Science-Based Benefits of Meditation*. Healthline. https://www.healthline.com/nutrition/12-benefits-of-meditation

Tiffany. (2016, June 17). *Food and Chakra Pairing: Balancing and Healing Our Energy Centers Through Food*. Parsnips and Pastries. https://www.parsnipsandpastries.com/chakra-food-pairing-balancing-healing-energy-centers-food/

Tracy, J. (2019, September 18). *7 Chakras Healing Foods | Chakra Food Chart*. 7 Chakra Store. https://7chakrastore.com/blogs/news/healthy-chakras-chakra-healing-foods

Wisdom by Gurudev. (2016, July 18). *Music & Chakras*. Wisdom by Sri Sri Ravi Shankar. https://wisdom.srisriravishankar.org/music-chakras/

Yoga in Daily Life. (n.d.-a). *Bhujangasana*. Www.Yogaindailylife.org. Retrieved December 12, 2020, from https://www.yogaindailylife.org/system/en/level-5/bhujangasana

Yoga in Daily Life. (n.d.-b). *Chakrasana*. Www.Yogaindailylife.org. Retrieved December 12, 2020, from https://www.yogaindailylife.org/system/en/level-6/chakrasana

Yoga in Daily Life. (n.d.-c). *Setu Asana*. Www.Yogaindailylife.org. Retrieved December 12, 2020, from https://www.yogaindailylife.org/system/en/level-2/setu-asana

Yoga in Daily Life. (n.d.-d). *Shalabhasana*. Www.Yogaindailylife.org. Retrieved December 12, 2020, from https://www.yogaindailylife.org/system/en/level-5/shalabhasana

Yoga in Daily Life. (n.d.-e). *Yoga Mudra*. Www.Yogaindailylife.org. Retrieved December 12, 2020, from https://www.yogaindailylife.org/system/en/level-6/yoga-mudra

Yoga Journal. (2007a, August 28). *Boat Pose*. Yoga Journal.
https://www.yogajournal.com/poses/full-boat-pose

Yoga Journal. (2007b, August 28). *Seated Forward Bend*. Yoga Journal. https://www.yogajournal.com/poses/seated-forward-bend

Yoga Journal. (2017a, April 12). *Plow Pose*. Yoga Journal.
https://www.yogajournal.com/poses/plow-pose

Yoga Journal. (2017b, April 17). *Staff Pose*. Yoga Journal.
https://www.yogajournal.com/poses/staff-pose

Yoga Journal. (2017c, May 16). *Supported Shoulderstand (Salamba Sarvangasana) - Yoga Journal*. Www.Yogajournal.com.
https://www.yogajournal.com/poses/supported-shoulderstand

Yoga Journal. (2019a, January 7). *Bharadvaja's Twist*. Yoga Journal. https://www.yogajournal.com/poses/bharadvaja-s-twist#section_4

Yoga Journal. (2019b, January 7). *Big Toe Pose*. Yoga Journal. https://www.yogajournal.com/poses/big-toe-pose

Yoga Journal. (2019c, January 7). *Bound Angle Pose (Baddha Konasana) - Yoga Journal*. https://www.yogajournal.com/poses/bound-angle-pose

Yoga Journal. (2019d, January 7). *Camel Pose*. https://www.yogajournal.com/poses/camel-pose

Yoga Journal. (2019e, January 7). *Child's Pose*. Yoga Journal. https://www.yogajournal.com/poses/child-s-pose

Yoga Journal. (2019f, January 7). *Cow Face Pose*. Yoga Journal. https://www.yogajournal.com/poses/cow-face-pose

Yoga Journal. (2019g, January 7). *Eagle Pose*. Yoga Journal. https://www.yogajournal.com/poses/eagle-pose

Yoga Journal. (2019h, January 7). *Firefly Pose*. Yoga Journal. https://www.yogajournal.com/poses/firefly-pose

Yoga Journal. (2019i, January 7). *Fish Pose*. Yoga Journal. https://www.yogajournal.com/poses/fish-pose

Yoga Journal. (2019j, January 7). *Hero Pose*. Yoga Journal. https://www.yogajournal.com/poses/hero-pose

Yugay, I. (2019, January 27). *How To Identify & Heal Blocked Chakras*. Mindvalley Blog. https://blog.mindvalley.com/symptoms-of-blocked-chakras/

Zoldan, R. J. (2020, June 22). *Your 7 chakras, explained—plus how to tell if they're blocked*. Well+Good. https://www.wellandgood.com/what-are-chakras/

Printed in Great Britain
by Amazon